THE COLI

General Editor:
Patrick McNeill

Auth

SOCIETY
NOW

Research Methods

Patrick McNeill

RESEARCH
METHODS

Tavistock Publications · London · New York

First published in 1985 by
Tavistock Publications Ltd
11 New Fetter Lane,
London EC4P 4EE
Reprinted 1986

Published in the USA by
Tavistock Publications
in association with Methuen, Inc.
29 West 35th Street,
New York, NY 10001

Printed in Great Britain by
Richard Clay Ltd,
Bungay, Suffolk

*British Library Cataloguing in
Publication Data*

McNeill, Patrick.
Research methods. – (Society now) –
(Social science paperback; no. 300)
1. Sociology – Methodology
I. Title   II. Series   III. Series
301'.072   HM24

ISBN 0–422–79540–2

*Library of Congress Cataloging in
Publication Data*

McNeill, Patrick.
Research methods.
(Society now)
Bibliography: p.
Includes index.
1. Sociology – Methodology.
2. Social sciences – Methodology.
I. Title.   II. Series.
HM24.M37   1985
301'.072   85–4656

ISBN 0–422–79540–2 (pbk.)

Contents

Acknowledgements

The author and publishers would like to thank the following for permission to reproduce copyright material: in Figure 2 Questions in social surveys, Oxford University Press for extracts from A. H. Halsey *et al. Origins and Destinations*, 1980; A. D. Peters & Co. Ltd for extracts from J. M. and R. E. Pahl *Managers and Their Wives*, Penguin, 1971; George Allen & Unwin for extracts from J. and E. Newson *Infant Care in an Urban Community*, 1963 and S. Edgell *Middle-class Couples*, 1980; University of Chicago Press for extracts from H. S. Becker *et al. Boys in White*, 1961; Cambridge University Press for extracts from J. H. Goldthorpe *et al. The Affluent Worker in the Class Structure*, 1969; Hutchinson Publishing Group Ltd for Figures 3 and 5 reproduced from P. McNeill and C. Townley *Fundamentals of Sociology*, 1981, Figures 2 and 4; and Penguin Books Ltd for Figure 6 reproduced from P. Worsley (ed.) *Introducing Sociology*, 2nd edn 1977, p. 89 Figure 2 (© Peter Worsley and contributors 1970, 1977).

Preface

Good social science, like all science, is based on good evidence. That is why research methods are important. I hope that this book will help you to distinguish between good evidence and poor evidence, in sociology and in everyday life.

I have included a very large number of references to published studies. Some students may find this a bit daunting, but I would stress that you are not expected to read more than one or two yourself. It has taken me twenty years to have read this many, and you have not got that long. The reason for mentioning so many is that it helps you decide which ones look interesting, and also gives you a sporting chance of actually getting hold of a copy of at least one.

There are suggestions for study activities scattered throughout the book. They can be carried out either individually or in pairs or groups. Group work is often more valuable than individual work, and always more fun.

Lastly, I wish to thank the staff of St Albans College library, especially Joyce Omasta, for their help over the years. They provide a university-standard library service on FE college resources.

Patrick McNeill

1

Research methods in sociology

'What is sociology about?' is probably the question that sociologists are asked more often than any other. A reasonable reply might be that sociologists are interested in those aspects of human behaviour that are the result of the social context in which we live. They do not concentrate on features which are the result of our physical or biological makeup. Sociology stresses the patterns and the regularities of social life which is, most of the time, orderly and largely predictable.

The next question is then, typically, 'But what do you actually do?' and it is to this question that this book is addressed. While there is, as you may know, considerable variation and disagreement among sociologists, they are united in the conviction that argument that is based on sound evidence is superior to argument based on false evidence, limited evidence, or no evidence. Evidence has to be collected from the social world around us, and this requires empirical research to be done. 'Empirical', in this context, simply means 'based on evidence from the real world' in contrast to 'theoretical', which refers to ideas that are abstract or purely analytical. A theory remains theoretical until it is tested against the real world, with empirical evidence. This still leaves open the question of what counts as sound evidence, and this in turn leads to a central theme of this book: 'How can we collect sound evidence about the social world that can be used to increase our understanding of that world?'

Over the years, sociologists have used a wide variety of methods of data collection and analysis. They have studied an even wider variety of aspects of social life, from such matters as how people avoid bumping into each other in the street to topics as wide-ranging as the causes of the rise of capitalism. In fact, a history of sociology since the end of the last century is an effective way of introducing the variety of research styles, and some of the topics studied.

The late nineteenth century

Modern sociology is usually thought to have its roots in the work of classical sociologists who worked at the end of the nineteenth and the beginning of the twentieth century. These writers, of whom Marx (1818–83), Weber (1864–1920), and Durkheim (1858–1917) are usually regarded as the most important, were essentially theorists, who based their analysis of what was happening to the rapidly changing European societies of that time on evidence from historians and other sources rather than on their own original research. In using such sources, they relied largely on what has come to be known as the 'comparative method'. This is a common, everyday method of explaining things. If, for example, we find that the flowers in one corner of the garden do better than those in another corner, we make various comparisons between the two sites, and perhaps reach the conclusion that it is the lack of sunshine on the second site that is causing those flowers to do so badly. The comparative method in sociology will be discussed in chapter 3, but essentially consists of the sociologist assembling data about several societies or social contexts and comparing them with each other, with the intention of explaining the causes of any variations. There is nothing very remarkable about this method of argument, but it forms the basis of modern scientific procedure.

At about the same time, i.e. the end of the nineteenth century, Charles Booth (1840–1916) was conducting one of the first major social surveys, which he published between 1891 and 1903 in seventeen volumes entitled *Life and Labour of the People in London*. Booth, prompted by a number of newspaper and magazine articles, was concerned to find out the true extent of poverty among the working classes of London at that time, and he collected vast quantities of data about them, using a combination of survey techniques and other less statistical methods. In his survey, he went from house to house in certain areas of the East End of London, painstakingly recording the number of residents, the number of rooms they occupied, their living conditions, their income, diet, clothing, and so on. He also collected their own accounts of the experience of poverty and their feelings about it. He spent some time actually living as a boarder in houses in the areas that he was studying, and making detailed studies of particular families.

Anthropology and the Chicago School

The first third of the twentieth century also saw the development of anthropological fieldwork. Researchers who were interested in the way of life of what were regarded as primitive peoples went to live among them to study their societies from the inside. Previously, investigations like this had been done mainly from the outsider's point of view, and it was men like Evans-Pritchard (1902–73), Radcliffe-Brown (1881–1955), and, particularly, Malinowski (1884–1942), who determined that the only really effective way of understanding the way of life of these peoples was to go and live among them for an

3

extended period of time, learning their language, and becoming accepted as a member of their social groups. Thus Evans-Pritchard's work on the magic and religion of the Azande, and on the political systems of the Nuer, and Malinowski's investigations among the Trobriand islanders established a new style and standard for this kind of academic scholarship. The methods that they developed, which are discussed in greater detail in chapter 4, are now used with many kinds of social groups, whether in the researcher's own society or elsewhere.

Another very important school of sociological research developed under the influence of Robert E. Park (1864–1944) at the University of Chicago in the period between the two world wars. They based almost all their work on anthropological techniques, but they were interested in the wide variety of life styles that they found on their own doorsteps in Chicago, not in simple societies. They used a method that became known as 'participant observation', in which the researcher both observes the social processes of a group and actually participates in the life of that group. They combined this with interviewing, some taking of life-histories, and the use of various official records and other documents. In this way, these researchers built up a picture of life styles in Chicago at that time, especially those of certain deviant groups such as hoboes and gang-members. They felt that a much truer picture of people's lives could be obtained by these methods of data collection than by the more formal survey, though they knew full well that all methods had something to contribute to sociological understanding.

Postwar research

After the Second World War, there was a change of emphasis among sociologists concerning what research techniques produced the best data. Under the influence of researchers in America such as Paul Lazarsfeld (1901–70), greater emphasis was put on the need for proof and on the importance of data

4

being as objective as possible, i.e. that it should be free of any influence of the individual researcher who happened to collect it. It was argued that, using the right data-collection techniques, it should be possible to assemble information about the social world that is free of bias, and that could be analysed using the statistical techniques that had been developed. The emphasis in this work was on the collection of statistical data, i.e. in the form of numbers, rather than descriptions of particular ways of life. The intention was to uncover the causes of human social behaviour, often with a view to influencing social policy in order to reduce social problems and generally improve the quality of life. This approach was strongly influenced by the methods of natural science.

From Booth onwards, there has been a strong tradition of empirical social research in Britain, much of it concerned with studies of poverty and other matters of social welfare. This tradition was reinforced in the 1950s and 1960s by the American influence, but other traditions of research, such as participant observation, never disappeared. The emphasis was on surveys, but these were seldom conducted without any reference to other methods, and some of the most famous British work of this period, that done by the Institute of Community Studies, used a combination of data-collection techniques.

During the 1960s, there were great changes in sociology in Britain. There was a reaction against the kind of sociology that encouraged the survey style of social research, and a move towards participant observation and other fieldwork techniques, such as informal or 'unstructured' interviews. A fuller account of these debates will be given in chapter 7, but the core of the dispute, as far as research methods were concerned, centred on whether sociological data was best collected by the use of surveys and questionnaires, which were regarded by their supporters as scientific and so more reliable, or by fieldwork involving participant observation. The survey people stressed the importance of neutrality and objectivity in research, and the participant observation enthusiasts argued

5

that the essential thing about social life is what it means to those involved, and that the only valid way of getting at these meanings is to participate in the lives of those who shared them.

One of the first and most important results of this change of emphasis was the work done by the joint Department of Sociology and Anthropology at the University of Manchester in the mid-1960s. Sociologists had long been interested in why many working-class pupils did not do as well as middle-class children at school. Until the mid-1960s, studies of this had concentrated on surveys of the home backgrounds of the children. Hargreaves (1967) and Lacey (1970) undertook studies of schools from the inside, playing the role of observers who also participated in school life. They showed how the organization of the schools played a part in the failure of certain pupils, and how the institution of streaming was actually helping to produce the very attitudes which led to the failure of children placed in the lower streams.

For several years, in the late 1960s and the early 1970s, sociologists seemed to spend as much time and effort arguing about how they should be thinking about and studying the social world as they did in actually doing research. These disputes were once described as 'British sociology's wars of religion', and, while sociology emerged in the late 1970s as a stronger discipline than it had been previously, this was not a period which was very productive in the terms of sociology's public image. However, some excellent studies were done at this time, many using fieldwork techniques and participant observation rather than surveys.

In the last few years, there seems to have been an outbreak of peace in sociology's own particular wars. In research terms, this has shown itself in the way that it has become perfectly acceptable to use a wide variety of research techniques in one study, and to use different techniques for the study of different topics. This may seem blindingly obvious to the newcomer to the discipline, but there were very good reasons for the disputes that took place. The arguments that are now available to justify the use of particular methods are much more convincing than they used to be. At the same time, it should not be forgotten that some writers had been advocating the use of multiple methods for years:

'Let us be done with the arguments of participant observation versus interviewing – as we have largely dispensed with the arguments for psychology versus sociology – and get on with the business of attacking our problems with the widest array of conceptual and methodological tools that we possess and they demand'.

(Trow 1957 quoted in Burgess 1982)

Other methods of research

This short review of the changing styles of sociological research has inevitably left out a great deal, much of which will be discussed elsewhere in this book. For example, the well-established tradition of 'community studies', which involves a researcher or a team of researchers using a wide variety of methods to study a whole community, has been producing work in both Britain and the USA almost continuously since the 1920s. It has been relatively unaffected, in terms of output, by the changing fashions and styles outlined above. Furthermore, nothing has yet been said about all the research that does not depend on the collection of data by the sociologist (primary data) but instead makes use of secondary data – the wealth of material already available from other sources, such as government statistics, personal diaries, newspapers, and other kinds of information. These will be considered in chapter 6. From time to time, too, sociologists and social psychologists have devised experiments to test their ideas, and these will be considered in chapter 3, alongside the comparative method.

It is important, too, to be aware that sociologists, like all other researchers, do their work in the real world of limited time and resources. Choice of research methods is often decisively affected by choice of topic, and the amount of time, money, and work hours available. These points will be raised throughout this book, and we will return to them again in chapter 7.

What is research for?

Having started this chapter with two questions, we can now add a third. What is sociological research for? Why is it done at all?

Descriptive and explanatory research

Some research aims only to describe, in detail, a situation or set of circumstances. The writer wishes to do no more than add to our knowledge of the social world, for its own sake. Other research sets out to explain some social phenomenon. It starts off with a question to be answered or a problem to be solved. This may be a social problem or a sociological problem.

Social problems are those aspects of social life that cause private unhappiness or public friction, and are identified by those in power as needing some kind of social policy to deal with them. 'Social policy' refers to those actions of governments that have a direct effect on the welfare of the citizens of a country. This may mean providing income for certain groups of people, as through the British social security system. It may mean providing services, such as education or a health service, which are available to all, or the home help service, which is available to those judged to be most in need of it. Sociological research can provide government with the information needed to identify the size of a problem, and to plan a response to that problem. This does not mean that governments always take action when researchers identify a social problem, or act upon their findings. They are free to ignore social research, and often do.

A sociological problem is any aspect of social life that needs explaining. It may also be a social problem, but sociologists are just as interested in trying to explain 'normal' behaviour and events as they are in trying to explain the deviant or the abnormal. Much research is concerned only with increasing our knowledge of how societies work, and explaining patterns of social behaviour. It may have implications for social policy, but this is not the prime purpose.

The distinction between descriptive research and explanatory research is often very blurred. Any explanation requires description, and it is difficult, or perhaps impossible, to describe something without at the same time explaining it.

Action research

This term is used to describe research that is done when some reform or change has been introduced. Its purpose is to monitor the effect of the change and to decide whether it has achieved what it was supposed to achieve. Various methods are employed, but the researcher has to be closely involved in the introduction of the reform being studied.

For example, the Plowden Committee, which reported in 1967 on the state of Britain's primary schools, found that the educational standards of schools in certain, mainly urban, areas were far below those found elsewhere. They recommended a policy of 'positive discrimination' in favour of these areas and their schools. As a result, Educational Priority Areas (EPAs) were established, in which extra money was spent on better primary schools, more teachers, and more resources for primary classrooms. The idea was that, by raising the standards of these deprived areas, the children in them would be brought up to the levels of those in more privileged communities, and would then be able to compete with them on equal terms later in their educational careers. The same thinking lay behind 'Project Headstart' in the USA in the 1960s.

When EPAs were introduced, they were systematically monitored by those involved. After a few years, the conclusion was reached that the experiment had not worked as it had been

9

expected to, and cuts in educational spending soon brought it to an end. Interestingly, exactly the same fate befell 'Project Headstart'.

Choice of research topic

This is affected by many things, most of which are to do with the interests and the values of the researcher, which are usually interrelated. Peter Townsend has had a life-long commitment to the needs of the poor and the powerless, and his studies of the elderly (1957) and the poor (1979) are the result of that commitment. Researchers will also be influenced by current debates in the academic world. Thus Goldthorpe and Lockwood (1969) carried out their research among the manual workers of Luton at a time when academic opinion was saying that such people were beginning to take on middle-class characteristics. Hannah Gavron made her study of housebound wives (1966) just at the start of the recent growth of feminist research, and in fact was a pioneer of that kind of research.

Choice of topic will also be affected by the funding of the research. Researchers who depend on grants from organizations like the Economic and Social Research Council, or from private foundations like the Gulbenkian, Ford or Joseph Rowntree, will only be able to carry out their enquiry if it is approved by the organization in question. Academic researchers working in higher education have to convince the relevant committees in their institution that the work is important enough for scarce resources to be devoted to it. Sometimes research is commissioned, and the researcher is approached by government, local authority, business, or charitable organization to carry out a specific enquiry on their behalf. Broadly speaking, it is easier to obtain funding for explanatory research that seems to provide guidance to policy-makers than for purely academic research, and for research that is statistically based than for research that is more qualitative in its approach. The choice of research topic is not made in a vacuum, but is influenced both by the researcher and by the context in which the research is to be done.

This does not automatically mean that the research is biased. Just because researchers have strong feelings about what they are investigating, it does not automatically follow that their findings will be slanted in favour of their own beliefs and values. Indeed, this is a major difference between social science and journalism. The social scientist must conduct a fair and balanced enquiry, not allowing personal or political values to affect what is discovered and reported. Values will influence the choice of topic, as they do in all branches of science, but methods should be value-free. Whether this is actually possible is a discussion we will return to in chapter 7.

Halsey, Heath, and Ridge (1980) say:

'(Booth ... the Webbs ... Mayhew ...) were concerned to describe accurately and in detail the social conditions of their society, particularly of the more disadvantaged sections, but their interest in these matters was never a disinterested academic one. Description of social conditions was a preliminary to political reform. They exposed the inequalities of society in order to change them. The tradition thus has a double intent: on the one hand it engages in the primary sociological task of describing and documenting the "state of society"; on the other hand it addresses itself to central social and political issues. It has never, therefore, been a "value-free" academic discipline, if such were in any event possible. Instead, it has been an attempt to marry a value-laden choice of issue with objective methods of data collection.'

It is also worth remembering that choice of topic is affected by the power of the subjects of the research to resist the investigation. How far such resistance is possible varies according to the research methods employed but, generally speaking, we know more about the poor and the powerless than we do about the rich and the powerful.

11

The textbook and the real world

In reading this book, you will find that the various research methods are described and explained one at a time. This is unavoidable, but it means that you may get the impression that they are also used one at a time. This is not the case. Every study uses more than one method, though there is often a strong preference for either survey-style research or participant observation.

Another problem with a textbook description of research methods is that the textbook gives the impression that this is what really goes on. It is not, any more than is the case in natural science. We will return to this point in chapter 7 but, for the moment, you should remember that the real world is always much untidier than the world of the textbook.

Three important concepts

Three key concepts are used throughout this book. Their meanings will become clear with use, but it is sensible to introduce them briefly at this stage.

Reliability

If a method of collecting evidence is reliable, it means that anybody else using this method, or the same person using it at another time, would come up with the same results. The research could be repeated, and the same results would be obtained. For example, an experiment in a chemistry lesson should always 'work'. It should always produce the result that is expected, whoever is doing it, at whatever time, provided that the proper procedures are followed.

Some methods in sociology are regarded as being more reliable than others. Any method that involves a lone researcher in a situation that cannot be repeated, like much participant observation research, is always in danger of being thought unreliable.

Validity

Validity refers to the problem of whether the data collected is a true picture of what is being studied. Is it really evidence of what it claims to be evidence of? The problem arises particularly when the data collected seems to be a product of the research method used rather than of what is being studied.

Suppose we were making an enquiry into people's leisure habits. If we designed a questionnaire to ask people what they did in their free time, how would we know whether the answers we received gave us a true picture of how they spend that time, or a picture of what they will say to a researcher when they are asked the question? This is not just a matter of people telling lies. They may genuinely believe what they are saying, but actual observation of what they do might well produce a different picture.

This is always a nagging doubt about any survey-style research. It must be accepted that what we are collecting is people's answers to questions, which is not necessarily a true picture of their activities. In laboratory experiments, we may be getting a picture of how people behave in laboratories, but can we be sure that this is how they behave in the real world (see p. 47)?

Representativeness

This refers to the question of whether the group of people or the situation that we are studying are typical of others. If they are, then we can safely conclude that what is true of this group is also true of others. We can generalize from the example that we have studied. If we do not know whether they are representative, then we cannot claim that our conclusions have any relevance to anybody else at all. As we shall see in chapter 2, careful sampling methods have been devised to try to ensure representativeness in survey research, but many other methods do not involve sampling, and there must always be a question as to the representativeness of their findings and conclusions.

13

Activity

Draw up a chart showing the history of sociological research since the end of the nineteenth century. On a large sheet of paper, mark the dates, at ten-year intervals from 1890 to 1990, on a scale along the longer side of the paper. Using the account given in this chapter, write names, dates, events, research styles, etc. Where they cover a period of time, use arrows to show the beginning and end. In some cases, this will go off the edge of the paper. In many cases, there will be overlap, so you can put things one above another.

Add to this chart as you work through this book.

2

Social surveys

Opinion polls and market research

A popular image of the social researcher is of a figure armed with a clipboard who approaches you in the street, and asks if you have the time to answer a few questions. If you agree to be questioned, there is a good chance that the questions will be on your political opinions, your voting intentions, or on your preferences with regard to washing powders, or foreign holidays, or TV programmes, or any of a host of other possibilities. These all come under the general heading of 'public opinion polls', and can take many forms.

Polls about people's voting intentions will usually be carried out by one of the big agencies such as MORI, Gallup, or National Opinion Polls. They are commissioned by the major political parties, by TV companies or by newspapers, to test public opinion on the major political issues of the day. The results are then made public and are used by whichever party

15

emerges with the most support from the poll. These polls have come to play an increasingly important part in the election process. In the period just before an election, results are published from some polling organization almost every day. The question asked is usually along the lines of: 'If the election were tomorrow, which party would you vote for?', and the results are then used to make predictions about the outcome of the election itself.

The pollster who asks you about washing powders or foreign holidays is probably working for a 'market research' organization. Their job is to find out what people are looking for when they spend their money, and to advise manufacturers and providers of services what the customer wants. This research forms an important part of the preparation and planning of any large commercial organization: it is conducted at several stages of the planning of a new product or service, and has reached a very high level of sophistication and accuracy. It is possible for research to find out, for example, where people would most like to go for their holidays, and how much they could afford to spend. The holiday firm then plans several possible packages, and conducts another poll inviting people to choose between them, or to express some other preference. Once they think they have a clear idea of which holiday would sell best to the public, they promote and market it. When a number of people have taken that holiday, they may conduct another poll to investigate whether they enjoyed it, and, most important, whether they would repeat it or recommend it to friends. The point is that very few firms now invest large sums of money in a new venture unless they are very sure that there is a demand for it. They may, of course, be wrong, and will then lose money, but market research is supposed to reduce the financial risks to a minimum.

While both the above are certainly types of social research, we will say no more about them here, since their specialist activities are not our major concern. What they have in common with sociological research, however, is that they depend for the accuracy of their results on choosing the right people to ask, and on having the right questions to ask them.

Social surveys

A social survey is a method of obtaining large amounts of data, usually in a statistical form, from a large number of people in a relatively short time. It has for many years been the most widely used method of social research. It may be explanatory or descriptive, or a combination of these. For example, the investigations into poverty carried out by Peter Townsend (1957, 1979) have been both descriptive and explanatory, and have been intended to prompt governments into modifying their policies in relation to the poor.

Stages in a survey

Figure 1   The stages in a survey

 1 Choice of topic to be studied
 2 Forming of hunches and hypotheses
 3 Identification of the population to be surveyed
 4 Carrying out preparatory investigations and interviews
 5 Drafting the questionnaire or interview schedule
 6 Conducting a pilot survey
 7 Finalizing the questionnaire
 8 Selecting a sample of the population
 9 Selection and training of interviewers (if necessary)
10 Collecting the data
11 Processing the data and analysing the results
12 Writing the research report, perhaps in the form of a book
13 Publication of the report

Figure 1 lists the stages of a social survey. It must be stressed again that there is always a difference between what text-books say and what real research is actually like. The stages are listed here not because this is exactly what every survey is like, or should be like, but because survey researchers have to

17

consider all these points at some stage, and usually in roughly this order. To develop an understanding of what survey research is actually like, you should read studies in the original. (For some suggestions, see p. 40.) Even when you have done this, you may not have the whole story, as is discussed on pp. 120–21.

We will now consider each stage in turn.

Choice of topic to be studied Some of the reasons why researchers choose their topics have been discussed on p. 10, but there are others which are peculiar to the survey. The main one is that certain topics simply cannot be studied in this way. Many historical themes are an example, since no respondents (people who answer the questions) are available. Illiterate people cannot be given a questionnaire, though they may, of course, be interviewed. A study of the distribution of power in society as a whole could hardly use the survey method, for who would be questioned and what questions could be asked? People who have something to hide, such as criminals or deviants, or even ordinary school pupils, may deliberately give untrue answers in order to protect themselves. The link between choice of topic and choice of method is considered again on p. 117.

Forming of hunches and hypotheses Whether the researcher recognizes it or not, this stage is inevitable. If researchers have absolutely no hunches at all about what they are going to find, how can they possibly know what questions to ask? Imagine an investigation into the causes of unemployment. Why does the researcher not include in the questionnaire a question about the person's favourite brand of cigarette? And does include a question about their educational achievement? The answer must be because the researcher assumes that cigarette smoking has nothing to do with unemployment, while educational achievement may have. In this example, the assumption is probably true, but if the question about cigarettes is not asked, then there is no chance that the researcher could ever discover

18

that they are a factor. Should a question be included about the number of children in the unemployed person's family? This just might be relevant. But if all 'might be relevant' questions were included, the questionnaire would be hopelessly long.

Sometimes the researcher will present an explicit hypothesis and set out to test it. An hypothesis is an informed guess about what the researcher thinks may be happening, based on previous research and observation. If this is done, then the choice of which questions to ask becomes much more clear cut (see p. 42). Often, however, a survey is more cautious and exploratory, and ideas are not firm enough to generate a specific hypothesis.

The point to remember is that any hunch, whether formally expressed as a hypothesis or not, is going to affect the general approach of the researcher and what questions are asked.

Identification of the population to be surveyed In some cases, this will be easy. If we are interested in the political opinions of young people, then all we have to do is to decide what age group we are interested in, and our population consists of all those people. If we wish to investigate the political opinions of students in higher education, then that is our population.

But what if we want to investigate the impact that a new motorway has had on the surrounding area? Who do we ask? Everybody who lives in the area? Including the children aged four or five? Should we include people who have moved away because of the motorway? If so, how can we identify and trace them? Perhaps we should include people who work in the area but do not live there? Should we not include people who regularly travel through the area by car, who must have an opinion about the difference it has made to their journey? And what about the local shopkeepers, or owners of cafés and petrol-stations? Should they not be investigated as a special category of people affected? How big an area are we going to investigate? Will we not have to make a decision in advance of what the extent of the motorway's influence has been?

You may think that you have answers to all these questions, and no doubt you have. What you must recognize is that the answers given to the questions will affect the outcome of the research. It follows that, when reading the reports of studies such as this, it is essential to be clear about the choices that the researcher made when deciding on the population to be surveyed.

Activity

Specify the survey population for studies of the following topics:
   (a) whether the merger of two schools has been a success;
   (b) relations between police and young people;
   (c) the causes of child-battering.

Carrying out preparatory investigations and interviews   This is not always done, but some researchers, aware of the problems outlined in the discussion on forming hunches and hypotheses above, spend time at this early stage in conducting informal interviews with people in order to find out from them what the key issues are. For example, if a researcher wants to investigate the factors that influence pupils when they are choosing the subjects they wish to study at higher levels of education, then group discussions with, for example, fourteen-year-old pupils in almost any urban school would give some ideas about what questions to include in a questionnaire. The researcher could not draw any generally valid or reliable conclusions from such discussions, but they should provide useful guidelines as to what areas should be followed up in the main enquiry.

Drafting the questionnaire or interview schedule   A questionnaire is a list of questions to be asked by the researcher. It is prepared in such a manner that the questions are asked in exactly the same way of every respondent. A questionnaire may be administered in a face-to-face situation, or may be sent through the post, or included in, for example, a newspaper or magazine, when it will be completed by the respondent without any supervision or guidance.

An interview schedule will always be administered face to face. It may be like a questionnaire, leaving the interviewer no discretion as to how to ask the questions or in what order. It is then referred to as a 'standardized interview'. More usually, it will allow the interviewer some flexibility and discretion, within a framework that is similar on every occasion. Where the form and order of an interview is left very much to the interviewer, we are dealing with an 'unstructured interview'. These will be discussed in more detail in chapter 3 (p. 68). Interview schedules can fall anywhere on a scale from the completely structured to the completely unstructured, and many include questions of several types within the same schedule. The structured interview will be favoured by the researcher who attaches great importance to the objectivity of the research, and who wishes to produce entirely statistical data.

When deciding what questions to ask, the researcher's first problem is usually to 'operationalize' the concepts he wishes to use. As so often in sociology, this rather alarming-sounding process is really very simple, though difficult to do well.

The problem is that most of the things that sociologists are interested in are abstract. They are concepts rather than actual objects. If I want to count how many chairs there are in my college, I have little problem about deciding which of the many objects in college I am going to include in my count. If, on the other hand, I want to count how many working-class students there are in the college, I cannot just go ahead and do it. I have to decide what I mean by 'working-class', and then I have to choose an 'indicator' of this concept. This indicator must be a characteristic that is easily identifiable, and which clearly distinguishes working-class students from others. Most sociologists faced with this particular problem have used occupation as the indicator. In most cases, they have produced social class scales which put professional people at the top, then other non-manual workers, then various grades of manual worker. They do not claim that occupation is the same thing as social class, but rather that it is the best single indicator of all those aspects of a person that make up their social class position. For a number of examples of social class scales of this type, see Reid (1981), especially chapter 2.

Argyle (1959) wanted to make a study of religious behaviour. As he says:

'Some people are more religious than others; what is required is some scale along which people who are more or less active can be distributed. Furthermore, the religious activity and beliefs of people take different forms, so that a number of different scales will probably be needed.'

He suggests some possibilities:

'Church membership is a widely used index. As an index it is rather unsatisfactory since it tells us very little about how active a person is or what he believes .... Frequency of church attendance is another valuable index. It has the advantage over membership that its significance is the same for different dates and denominations. On the other hand, it may be argued that the Catholic Church puts on greater pressure for sheer attendance than some other churches. There may be some people who simply observe the outward forms of religion, in order to keep up appearances or not to upset their relations, but who have no real religious belief or feelings .... The saying of private prayers, and other forms of private religious behaviour, can be ascertained in answer to questions, but not validated against direct observations of behaviour .... Attitudes towards religion or the church provide another index.'

In every case, operationalization of the key concept in a research project has far-reaching consequences for the results of the research. For example, if we are trying to measure poverty, then our definition of poverty will actually produce the amount of it that we find. If we decide that poor people are those whose income falls below a certain specified level, then we will have to count all those who are in that category. But if we lower our 'poverty line', we will at the same time reduce the number of poor people, and if we raise it, we will increase the number. And that is likely to have serious implications for government policy.

Activities

1 Operationalize the following concepts:
   (a) educational failure;
   (b) overcrowding (of private home);
   (c) loneliness.

2 Now find out how overcrowding is operationalized in government statistics. You will need to look these up in the *Housing Statistics*, published quarterly, or in a report from an organization like Shelter. How does this compare with your way of measuring overcrowding?

3 Now look at the Pelican (1963) version of Townsend's *The Family Life of Old People*, chapter 13. Compare his measuring of 'social isolation' with yours of 'loneliness'.

Once concepts have been operationalized, it is possible to begin drafting questions. The skills involved are so varied and complex that whole books have been written about it, and there is no chance of going into the topic in great depth here. There are, however, some points to be made.

Questionnaires may be made up of 'closed' or 'open' questions. With closed questions, the researcher has in some way limited the possible responses. For example, there may be a simple YES/NO/DON'T KNOW set of alternatives to choose from. Or there may be a list of possible answers, of which at least one must be ticked. The advantage of this method is that results can be presented in the form of statistics and tables. This requires that answers be precoded so that the responses can be fed straight into a computer which has been programmed to receive them. The problem is that the researcher has imposed a limit on the possible answers that the respondent may give, and this may cast doubt on the validity of the data collected.

With open questions the researcher leaves it to the respondents as to how they word their answers. Questions can therefore be more wide-ranging and open-ended. Such questions are more often asked in the interview situation than in a postal questionnaire. The interviewer may ask a question and follow it up with 'prompts' or 'probes' to encourage the respondents to go into more depth with their answers. There are, however, dangers in 'over-probing', which may put answers into respondents' heads.

Open questions make it possible for respondents to say what they really feel, but it is difficult for the researcher to organize the answers into categories in order to count them. With closed questions it is easier to count the replies and perform statistical operations on them, but it is difficult to get at what the respondent really thinks about something. Many interview schedules have a mix of the two types. They may start with closed questions about, for example, age or marital status, and move on to more open-ended questions as the interview progresses.

The wording of questions, especially closed questions and those asked in a postal questionnaire, must be clear, precise, and unambiguous. The language used should be as simple as possible. Questions must not presume that respondents have more knowledge than in fact they have, and must not lead respondents towards a particular answer. This is much more difficult than it sounds, and requires a great deal of skill and practice.

As an example of the pitfalls involved in drafting questions, we can consider the fuss that there was in 1983 when Hill announced that he had found that as many as 40 per cent of six-year-old children had seen 'video-nasties' (i.e. video films of horror, violence, and sadistic sex). In his questionnaire, he named some of the more famous such videos, and asked the children to say whether they had seen them. His findings produced a lively press response, and questions in the House of Commons, and certainly contributed to the passage of a bill through Parliament to limit the availability of such films. Cumberbatch and Bates repeated the research, asking another

24

sample of children, eleven-year-olds this time, whether they had seen certain such videos. They achieved a figure of 68 per cent of the children claiming to have seen these films. The point was, however, that Cumberbatch and Bates had named a number of video-nasties that did not in fact exist, and yet the children claimed that they had seen them. What Hill had found was that children would claim to have seen video-nasties, rather than that they had actually seen them. This is a very good example of the validity problem referred to on p. 14 (for a fuller account see Harris 1984).

Figure 2   Questions in social surveys

Secondary schooling

I want to ask you about your schooling *after* the age of eleven. What schools did you go to then? (Any others?)

	circle all which apply
Stayed at exact same school	01
Elementary school	02
Central/Intermediate/Higher elementary/	
Senior school	03
All age school/Advanced division	04
Secondary modern/Junior secondary school/	
Vocational school (Republic of Ireland—South)	05
Comprehensive (including multilateral and bilateral	
schools	07
Technical school	07

⎧ Grammar school	08 ⎫	give
⎪ Direct grant/Grant aided	09 ⎪	name(s)
⎨ Independent (fee-paying) school	10 ⎬	and
⎩ Scotland only: senior secondary school	11 ⎭	location(s)
Scotland only: higher grade	12	
Republic of Ireland (South) only:		
'secondary' school	13	

Source: Halsey, Heath, and Ridge (1980)

Your marriage

(a) How did you meet your husband?

(b) What was the date of your marriage? ....
     How old were you then? ....
(c) How many children have you? ....
(d) And what are their ages? ....
(e) And how many more children do you *expect* to have? ....
(f) Ideally, how many children would you *like* to have? ....

Comment

(g) How do you see yourself now? Please tick one place on the
     following scale opposite each statement.
>   1 = Essentially so
>   2 = Very much so
>   3 = To a large extent
>   4 = To a certain extent
>   5 = Not really

Someone who is:	1	2	3	4	5	
1 Providing an interesting activity for your children.						1
2 Creating a comfortable and well-run home.						2
3 A companion to your husband.						3
4 Concerned with interests of your own, e.g. pottery.						4
5 Keen to do a paid job now and again.						5
6 Keen to follow a career of your own.						6
7 Active in local clubs, church, or other organizations.						7
8 A friendly person in your neighbourhood.						8

Source: Pahl and Pahl (1971)

General background: husband

1 Age.
2 Born: (a) London, (b) St Pancras, (c) England, (d) other.
3 Educated: (a) elementary, (b) secondary modern, (c) grammar, (d) private.
4 Age left.
5 Parents alive.
6 Born: (a) London, (b) St Pancras, (c) England, (d) other.
7 Now living.
8 Occupation of father.
9 Social class.
10 Occupation of husband.
11 Wage.
12 Social class.
13 Enjoyed period between school and marriage; (a) yes, (b) no.
14 Comment on parents.

Source: Gavron (1966)

Father's participation in child-rearing

How much does his father have to do with him? Does he (mark each category: often (O), sometimes (S) or never (N))
Feed him? ....   Change him? ....   Play with him? ....
Bath him? ....   Get him to sleep? ....
Attend to him in the night? ....
Take him out *without you*? ....
If there are other children: does father do a lot for some other child? ....
Have you got a washing machine? YES/NO
Do you and your husband ever manage to leave the baby so that you can both go out? YES/NO How often? ....
Does somebody come in to look after the baby?
Information wanted: (a) Paid baby-sitter/relative/friend/other children, (b) Stays in the house all evening/looks in occasionally/listens from elsewhere/nobody is responsible for the baby ....

Would you say you are bringing up your children the same way as you yourself were brought up, or differently? ....
....

Source: Newson and Newson (1963)

---

1 In our society some people claim that equality between the sexes has been achieved. Do you agree? ....
2 Would you briefly explain why you agree or disagree in Question 1 above ....
    ....
    ....
    ....
3 Do you think that equality between the sexes in all walks of life is a good thing or a bad thing? ....
4 Would you briefly explain why you think that equality between the sexes is a good or bad thing? ....
    ....
    ....
• 5 How do you regard domesticity? Please delete any inappropriate words. Easy/difficult/boring/interesting/worthwhile/waste of time/enjoyable/unenjoyable/satisfying/unsatisfying.
6 Whose company do you prefer most? Please delete any inappropriate words. Relatives/friends/professional colleagues/males/females.
7 If you were granted three wishes, what would you wish for? Please be as specific as possible and put them in order of importance.
    (a) ....
    (b) ....
    (c) ....
Please try and answer all the following questions as frankly as possible. This is of the highest importance if the survey findings are to be valid. There are no 'right' or 'wrong' answers. Please indicate your answers by marking the response which most accurately fits your own experience.
1a Do you and your mate agree on how your children should be brought up? Always agree/almost always agree/occasionally agree/occasionally disagree/almost always disagree/always agree.

2a Do you and your mate agree on the type of education your children should receive? Always agree/almost always agree/occasionally agree/occasionally disagree/almost always disagree/always disagree.

3a Do you and your mate agree on the subject of contraception? Always agree/almost always agree/occasionally agree/occasionally disagree/almost always disagree/always disagree.

Source: Edgell (1980)

---

59 Do you think your training will be good enough for you to be able to handle everything you should or will as a GP?

60 Do you think you will be ready to go out and practise medicine on your own after you finish school and do a year of internship?

61 What kind of a car should a doctor drive?

62 Do you think that being a medical student sort of separates you from other people?

63 Do you think being a doctor will?

64 What are the most important courses you're taking this year? What makes them important?

65 Which courses are least important? Why?

66 In each of the other years you have been in school, which courses were most important? Which least? Why?

67 Have your ideas changed about the relative importance of courses you had in earlier years? Why?

68 What thing(s) about your work this year has given you the most trouble?

69 What was your biggest single problem during your first months in medical school?

Source: Becker *et al.* (1961)

Section 2 The worker and his job

5 Hand card. Here are some of the things often thought important about a job. Which one would you look for first in a job? And which next?

Interest and variety

Good pay and the chance of plenty of overtime

Good workmates

A supervisor who doesn't breathe down your neck
Pleasant working conditions
A strong and active union

6 So far as these two things are concerned would you say that your present job is:
First rate?
Pretty good?
Not too good?
Very bad?

7 Do you find your present job physically tiring?

8 Would you say it puts a great strain on your nerves? *Prompt if necessary: 'Does it make you feel jittery at the end of the day?'*

9 Do you find it monotonous?

10 [Vauxhall] Can you 'work up the line' or 'build a bank' in your job?
    If 'No': Why is that?
    [Skefko] Do you set yourself an output target – say, so many pieces of work per day?
    If 'Yes': Do you ever work faster to get within reach of the target early on and then take it easy for a bit?
    [This question was not asked of Laporte workers.]

11 Do you ever find the pace of the job too fast?

12 Do you find you can think about other things while doing your job?
    If 'Yes': What do you think about?

13 Which would you prefer: a job where someone tells you exactly how to do the work or one where you are left to decide for yourself how to go about it?

Source: Goldthorpe and Lockwood (1969)

Activity

Study the examples of questions in *Figure 2*, all of which are taken from social surveys, both postal and face to face. Identify which questions are (a) open; (b) closed; (c) multiple-choice; (d) precoded. Which ones include prompts or probes? What changes would you make to any of the questions?

Before you get too critical, you should look at the questionnaires in the original.

Conducting a pilot survey   This stage of questionnaire-based research should never be omitted. In it, the researcher tries out the questionnaire on a number of people who are similar to those who will be investigated in the actual research. Any problems with the drafting, and perhaps the layout, of the questionnaire should show up at this stage and can be corrected before the real investigation starts.

Finalizing the questionnaire   At this point the researcher will produce a final version of the questionnaire, ready for use in the real investigation.

Activities

1 The following books include a copy of the full questionnaire that was used:
  Blauner (1964); Edgell (1980); Gavron (1966); Goldthorpe and Lockwood (1969); Goldthorpe (1980); Halsey *et al.* (1980); Newby (1977); Newson and Newson (1963); Pahl and Pahl (1971); Runciman (1966); Townsend (1957); Townsend (1979); Willmott and Young (1960); Young and Willmott (1973).
  Study the questions asked in at least two of these books. Are they open or closed? Are they precoded? Is there a mixture of types in any particular study?

2 The following questions were all produced by my students last year when I asked them to draft a questionnaire:
  Do you often read books?
  What are your favourite leisure activities?
  Have you been ill recently?
  What do you think of the help given to the physically handicapped?
  What is it like to have a mentally handicapped child?
    What is wrong with these questions? If you cannot tell, try them out on several people, and the problems will be clear. Now try to write questions of your own that will produce the information that my students seem to have wanted.

Selecting a sample of the population   In this context, the term 'population' refers to all those people who could be included in the survey. As we have already seen (p. 19), this may be quite clear, or it may require decisions to be made about who will be included and who will be omitted. Either way, the chances are that there will be a very large number of people, possibly several million, depending on the subject of the research, and there is no way that the researcher is going to be able to deliver a questionnaire to them all, still less interview them face to face. Accordingly, a sample has to be chosen.

We are all familiar with the idea of sampling. For example, when I go to the market to buy fruit, I will usually, despite what the stall-holder says, try to handle an apple or two from the display to see what they are like. If I am happy with their quality, I will ask for the quantity that I want. I assume that the quality of the ones I have handled is typical or representative of the quality of the others. When I dip my toe in the swimming pool before going in, I assume that the temperature of that part of the water is representative of the temperature of the whole pool.

Exactly the same principle applies when sampling for social research. The researcher aims to investigate a sample of the population, because this is cheaper and quicker, but the sample must be representative of the population as a whole. That is to say, what is true of the sample should be true of the population, or at least it should be possible to calculate the likelihood of its being true. There are various ways of selecting such a sample.

'Random' or 'probability' sampling is the one that most people are familiar with. The researcher first has to produce a 'sampling frame'. This is a list of the population concerned, organized into 'sampling units'. Choosing a sampling unit may itself be a problem. If we are interested only in individuals, it is a straightforward matter. But what if we want to investigate families? Or households? These will need to be defined, and then some means of assembling a list of them will have to be found.

However, let us assume that we are interested in individuals. There are various lists available for this purpose. If we are investigating adults, then a favourite sampling frame used by sociologists is the electoral roll. This is the list of all those in an area who are eligible to vote at elections. It is brought up to date each year, and includes virtually everybody over eighteen who is resident in a constituency. Doctors' lists are another favourite sampling frame.

If we are studying school-pupils in a certain area, then we might try to get hold of a list of all secondary school attenders from the local education office. If we are interested in young mothers, then we might try the Register of Births, and ask for a list of all recent births that have been registered.

Activity

Think of all the lists of names that might be available to researchers. For example, the telephone directory, sports club membership lists, college students lists, school rolls, lists of employees, etc. Consider the value of each one as a sampling frame.

Such lists are not always easy to find, as is described by Newby (1977) when he tried to devise a sampling frame of farms in a certain area. They may not exist or access to them may be refused. Pearson (1981) found:

'In common with previous studies of ethnic minorities in Britain, it proved difficult to find a suitable sampling frame .... Electoral registers, street directories, etc., were either inappropriate (these lists do not indicate birth-place or nationality) or unavailable (for example, Council housing or rating lists). A sample was finally constructed by using the files of a local vicar and a list of West Indian parents which was obtained from a local junior school.'

Activity

Obtain a copy of some of the books listed on p. 40 and see what their sampling frames were.

Once we have a sampling frame, we can select a certain number of names from it. If we choose names out of a hat, or by using random numbers, then we are doing truly random sampling. If we choose every tenth or every twentieth name, then this is called quasi-random sampling, since not every name on the list has an equal chance of being chosen.

Stratified sampling works slightly differently. It is always possible, though unlikely, that a random sample will, by chance, include a higher proportion of one group of people than there should be for it to be truly representative. If a town has 10,000 residents over twenty-one, of whom exactly half are male and half female, a random sample of one tenth of them is unlikely to produce exactly half men and half women, and it might produce a very biased sample of, say, 650 women and 350 men. To avoid this possibility, we can opt for a stratified sample. In this case, we would divide our population into men and women, and then take a 10 per cent sample of each of these groups. In this way, we would be guaranteed to produce 500 men and 500 women. If we wanted further to stratify the sample to allow for age distribution, we could do this too, by dividing the men and the women into age groups, and taking one tenth of each of the resulting groups.

Quota sampling is like stratified sampling, but with an important variation. In this case, the researcher decides how many of each category of person should be included in the sample, but then, instead of selecting them at random from a sampling frame, the researcher goes out looking for the right number of people in each category until the quota is filled. Thus if, in a sample of 500 people, the quota of women aged between thirty and forty is twenty-two, the researcher will look out for twenty-two such women and, when they have been found and interviewed, that is the quota filled. This method is most often used by market researchers, but is not unknown among sociologists.

Multi-stage sampling just means drawing one sample from another. If we wanted a national sample of school-children, we could draw a sample of education authorities, then draw a sample of schools from each of those, then a sample of children from each school.

'Purposive sampling' occurs when a researcher chooses a particular group or place to study because it is known to be of the type that is wanted. Goldthorpe and his team (1969) wanted to study manual workers with high incomes to see whether they had developed a middle-class way of life. They decided to study a group of workers in Luton because they were known to have high incomes. Goldthorpe thought that, if they had not adopted a middle-class way of life, then it was unlikely that any other working-class people had done so.

There are various other kinds of sampling procedure, and any statistics textbook will explain them. Another one you may come across is known as 'snowball' sampling. This is much less systematic than the others described above, and has little claim to be representative at all. It involves identifying certain key individuals in a population, interviewing them, and then asking them to suggest others who might also be interviewed. In this way, the original small nucleus of people grows by adding people to it in stages, much as a snowball can be built up by rolling it along the snow on the ground.

Selection and training of interviewers (if necessary) If there are large numbers of people to be interviewed, it will be necessary to select and train a team of people to act as assistant interviewers. The idea is that all the interviews should be conducted in as similar a way as possible, and that the dangers of 'interviewer effect' should be avoided by training. Interviewers have to strike a careful balance between establishing the kind of relationship with respondents that will encourage them to be frank and truthful, and avoiding becoming too friendly so that respondents try hard to please. 'Friendly but restrained' is a phrase often used to describe this attitude, and interviewers are usually encouraged to be as non-directive as possible. Becker, on the other hand, who tends to use a more open-ended style of interviewing, has argued that the interviewer should sometimes 'play dumb' and pretend not to understand what is being said, in order to prompt the respondent into saying more.

Assistant interviewers must be chosen with care. Willmott (1966) chose to use young Australians and New Zealanders in his research into the activities of adolescent boys, on the assumption that they would be seen by the boys as neutral as far as class and social background were concerned. The Newsons, in their study of child-rearing in Nottingham (1963), used health visitors to conduct some of their interviews. They found that young mothers seemed to give health visitors a more idealized version of how they treated their babies than the account they gave to Elizabeth Newson, who was not seen to have any authority over them.

All researchers have to think carefully about whether the interviewer's sex, class, race, or accent will affect the answers that are given. No amount of training can overcome problems like this.

Collecting the data   As we have seen, a questionnaire can be sent by post or administered face to face. Occasionally, a simple questionnaire may even be administered by telephone.

Money is usually important. Postal questionnaires are cheap to administer, and can cover very large numbers of people. Face-to-face interviews take time and cost much more in relation to the number of respondents interviewed.

There are several issues here. The first is the question of the 'response rate', which refers to the number of people who actually complete and return the questionnaire. This is the major drawback of the postal method, where response rates, usually around 30–40 per cent, are lower than in face-to-face research, which can hope to achieve an 80 or even 90 per cent response. Those to whom the questionnaire is sent have already been carefully selected as representative of the population to be studied. If some or even most of them do not respond, how can we know whether the answers that we have got are representative? Did people refuse to co-operate, or were they uncontactable, having moved or died? If some kind of bias has been introduced, how can we know what it is? Are people who volunteer to answer questionnaires in some way different from those who refuse? Are such differences important for this particular piece of research? All researchers have a system of calling back to respondents, and some will, in the end, use replacements, but this is another potential problem area.

In the end there is no answer to this problem, and it is very important, when evaluating published research, to take note of the response rate, and to consider whether it is adequate.

Activity

Look at the response rates achieved in the surveys listed on p. 40. Are they adequate? How could they have been improved? What were the causes of non-response?

The second issue has two aspects: anonymity and confidentiality. With some research topics, such as asking people to say what criminal offences they have committed, the only chance of getting any truthful answers would be with a guarantee that the answers would be confidential (no one else would be told the answers given by a particular individual), and the best way of ensuring this is to allow respondents not to give their names (anonymity). This does not, of course, guarantee truthfulness, but it must improve the chance that the replies will be honest.

Where the interview is held may also affect the validity of the replies. In a survey of school-children, we might expect that the answers they give in an interview held in the headmaster's study will be different from those they give at home, or out of doors. If the interview is at all long, the respondent must be comfortable and have time to answer the questions carefully.

Occasionally a joint interview will be held, as in the research done by Pahl and Pahl (1971), which investigated the relationship between senior managers and their wives.

Lastly, there is the possibility of running group interviews. These are not very common and, as previously suggested, feature more often in preparatory work than in the actual research, but they do have a place. Of course, they will always involve open questions, and the results are almost impossible to express statistically. Cohen and Taylor (1972) used this technique, among others, in their study of long-term prisoners in the maximum security wing of a British prison.

Processing the data and analysing the results Having collected all the completed questionnaires or interview schedules, it is time to process the data, putting answers into categories, adding up totals, and generally finding out the pattern of the responses and expressing them in statistical terms. Nowadays, computers can play a crucial role in this. In fact, they have made it possible to process far greater amounts of data than ever before.

Writing the research report, perhaps in the form of a book This can be a very lengthy process, depending on the amount of work that has to be done on the data collected. It is rare for any substantial report to be published within less than two years of the end of the data-collection phase, and it is very often a great deal longer than this. Even if the researcher completes the writing within, say, a year, publishers need at least a year to publish the book.

Publication of the report Publication day is when the work becomes available to other social scientists. They will make judgements as to the quality of the work, basing their opinion upon what is actually published, and the author's reputation may be made or broken by what the critics say. This is an important aspect of research. It may be done partly for the love of the work, but every author is also concerned to establish a reputation for good work among those whose opinion matters.

Summary

The advantages and disadvantages of the survey technique of social research may be summarized as follows.

Advantages

Large numbers of people can be studied.

The method is relatively quick, and relatively cheap.

If the survey is properly conducted, the results are reliable, and representative of a much wider population than that directly investigated.

If the research is properly carried out, the personal influence of the researcher on the results is slight.

It produces data that can easily be expressed in statistical form. This enables comparisons to be made between different groups and populations.

Disadvantages

The interview is a very artificial situation. There is no guarantee that what people say in interviews is a true account of what they actually do, whether they are intentionally lying or whether they genuinely believe what they are saying. People are quite capable of saying one thing and doing another, and of being quite unaware of this. 'Interview effect' is as important as 'interviewer effect'. Oakley (1979) has a very interesting discussion of the effect that the interview has on the person doing the interview, as well as on the interviewee.

The interview schedule or questionnaire mean that the researcher is setting limits to what the respondent can say. The more structured the interview, the more this is the case. How can the researcher possibly know in advance what the important questions are? What if the multiple choice allowed in the questionnaire does not include the answer that the respondent wants to give?

It is unlikely that anyone will give full or truthful answers in an interview to questions that concern sensitive, embarrassing, or possibly criminal aspects of their lives.

Fundamentally, the survey method finds out what people will say when they are being interviewed or filling in a questionnaire. This may not be the same thing as what they actually think or do. There is therefore a major problem with the validity of the findings of such research.

Further reading

The books listed on p. 31 all include a reasonably full description of how their survey was carried out, as do the following:

    Bott (1971)   Oakley (1979)   Roberts et al. (1977)
    Schofield (1965) Willmott (1966) Young and Willmott
    (1957)

You cannot hope to read all of these, but see the suggestion on p. 73 about a group sharing the work.

If you can only read one, make it Young and Willmott (1957) or Schofield (1965). Notice how virtually every study makes use of more than one research technique.

Activities

1 Many students are encouraged to 'do' their own survey. I have reservations about this, which I outline in Gomm and McNeill (1982), Items 55 and 58. In brief, my objection is that a proper survey requires time, money, and resources, and that it is unfair on all concerned to do a lot of hard work on something that is sociologically worthless. Not everybody would agree with this view. Gomm and McNeill (1982) suggests several ways of simulating the research process.

2 Whenever you hear or read about the findings of a survey, in the newspaper, on TV, or in a sociology lesson, ask yourself, 'How could they possibly have found that out? Is that information reliable or valid?'

3

Experiments and the comparative method

When people think of natural scientists doing research, they tend to think of them in a laboratory, probably doing an experiment. The experiment is the classic research method of the natural scientist, and has produced many of its most valuable results. This is because the experiment is most suited to the assumptions that natural scientists have traditionally made about what they are studying. They assume that the natural world has an independent existence of its own, which is as it is regardless of those who are studying it, and which is governed by laws which can be discovered by the research scientist if only the right methods can be developed. The knowledge that is discovered using these methods is regarded as objective and factual, i.e. it is correct for all times and all places, and is not going to be different according to who discovers it. Once that knowledge is gained, it can be used to explain events in the natural world, to make predictions about what will happen in the natural world, and thus to control that world and make it behave in ways that are, at least in theory, to the advantage of the controllers. We will pursue this debate further in chapter 7 of this book, and find that this picture of natural science has been modified recently. For the moment, however, we will accept these assumptions.

The hypothetico-deductive method

This is the name given to the logic of the research method that natural science is thought to employ. It is illustrated in *Figure 3*. The process starts with the phenomena (1), out there in the world, which can be observed objectively. These almost casual observations prompt ideas in the mind of the scientist (2), from which is developed an hypothesis (3). This is essentially an intelligent guess about what is happening, but in a form that can be tested. This test may be done as an experiment in the laboratory, or by further data collection 'in the field'. The scientist should try to prove the hypothesis wrong. This is

Figure 3 The hypothetico-deductive method

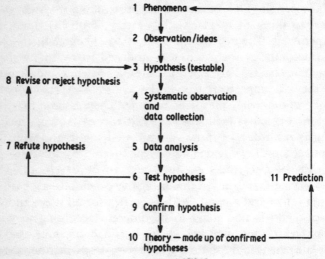

Source: McNeill and Townley (1981)

because, however often an experiment comes out right, you can never be sure that it will come out right the next time, and so you can never be sure that your hypothesis is right. It only has to come out wrong once for you to know that the hypothesis is wrong. An experiment is then carried out (or data is collected in the field) (4), and the results are analysed (5). The hypothesis is then tested against these results (6). If the hypothesis is not supported by the evidence (7), it can be rejected or revised (8), and a fresh hypothesis developed (3). If it is supported by the evidence (9), then it can be seen as a contribution to theory (10). If the theory becomes elaborate enough, it begins to look like a law, and predictions about future events may be made (11).

Let us illustrate this method with an example. Suppose a scientist is trying to find out what will improve milk yield in cows. Ordinary observation will suggest to the researcher that things like the type of grass available, additions to diet, the amount of water drunk, and the frequency of milking all play their part. These factors will be taken one at a time, and the scientist will set up experiments to test them. Being a scientist in a western society, the researcher is unlikely to think that music or magic have much influence.

The first hypothesis might be that 'milk yield is linked to the amounts of water cows drink and the intervals at which they drink it'. To test this, the experimenter must establish two groups of cows, the 'control group' and the 'experimental group'. Each group is matched in every possible way: species, age, health, etc. They will be put into identical environments which are controlled in every respect by the experimenter. The experimenter will then deliver a certain amount of water at regular intervals to the control group, but will systematically vary the amount of water delivered to the experimental group. If the milk yield of the experimental group varies, and the variation is linked to water intake, the experimenter is entitled to assume that there is a causal link between milk yield and water intake, since there is no other difference between the two groups. It would be a basic mistake to assume that the first correct answer is the only one that exists, so the scientist will conduct further experiments, trying all the time to prove the hypothesis wrong. If it cannot be proved wrong, then the scientist will conclude that there is a causal law in operation, and will advise farmers, who are likely to have paid for the research, of this.

The variable that is controlled by the experimenter is called the 'independent variable', and anything that varies as a result of this is called a 'dependent variable'. For example, the amount of fresh air for the cows might be the independent variable, and the milk yield would be the dependent variable.

To summarize: the purpose of the experiment is to create a standardized situation for the researcher to study, in which all variables are under the control of the experimenter, and in which the results of manipulating variables can be studied and measured. If some correlation is found between variables, the researcher has to show that this is a causal relationship rather than just a coincidence.

Activity

Make up an hypothesis, and design an experiment, about the following:
  (a) the growth of tomato plants;
  (b) wool yield in sheep;
  (c) lead poisoning in swans.

Laboratory experiments in social science

What relevance does this have for the social scientist? What aspects of human behaviour can be studied in the laboratory? What are the advantages of such an approach?

The laboratory method appeals to those who believe that, in the last analysis, human behaviour can be studied and explained in the same way as can events in the world of nature. There are assumed to be patterns of cause and effect that can be identified.

44

Laboratory experiments can only last for a relatively short time, and have to be held within the confines of the laboratory. As a result, most social science experiments have been carried out by psychologists rather than by sociologists, though many of their experiments overlap with the interests of sociology. An example of such work is that of Milgram (1965).

Milgram was interested in the effects of authority on human behaviour. He set up an experiment, in laboratory conditions, where volunteers were asked to co-operate in a 'learning experiment'. On arrival at the laboratory, they met a second volunteer and the research scientist. The volunteers drew lots as to who was to be 'teacher' and who to be 'learner', and the teacher saw the learner being strapped into a chair. The teacher was then taken into another room and shown an apparatus which could deliver electric shocks to the learner. It was labelled as being able to give shocks of up to 450 volts. The teacher, with a white-coated scientist standing by him, was then instructed to teach the learner a series of linked words, and to punish him by delivering a shock every time he made a mistake. The shocks were to be increased with each error. As the experiment continued the learner would begin to protest, scream, demand that he be released, and even hammer on the wall; eventually he would fall silent. The teacher was told by the researcher to regard silence as a wrong answer and to punish it accordingly. The level of shock being delivered was shown on the apparatus as being 'severe', 'dangerous', and, at the top end of the scale, just 'xxx'.

What the 'teacher' volunteer did not know was that the whole experiment was a set-up and that the 'learner' was in fact a co-worker of Milgram's. No electric shocks were actually being transmitted, and the experiment, rather than being about learning and punishment, was concerned with how far people would obey others who held an official or expert position.

Milgram found that twenty-six of his forty volunteers – 65 per cent – were prepared to administer the maximum shock to a stranger in these circumstances. Milgram varied the context of the experiment systematically, sometimes by allowing the 'teacher' to see the effects of the shocks on the 'learner', sometimes having them in the same room, sometimes not having the learner scream in pain, and so on. However, the general rule was that the closer, the more visible, or the more audible the learner was to the teacher, the fewer teachers were prepared to go all the way with the shocks. But even when the teacher had to hold the learner's hand on the electric shock plate, 30 per cent of the volunteers were prepared to do this. The physical presence of the supervisor was also found to be an important independent variable.

Another example of this type of research was reported by Haney, Banks, and Zimbardo (1973). In this case, a simulated prison was created and twenty-four volunteers were assigned to the roles of 'guard' or 'prisoner'. This was the independent variable, manipulated by the experimenters, and the dependent variable to be studied was the effect that these roles would have on the behaviour of the volunteers. After instruction in the regulations of the 'prison' the volunteers were placed in it for nearly a week, and their reactions and behaviour observed. The simulation was as total as possible, and the guards were told that the research interest was the behaviour of the prisoners.

The effects were dramatic. Five prisoners had to be released because of extreme emotional depression. The experiment had to be ended early because of the behaviour it was inducing in both guards and prisoners. Only two prisoners refused the offer of early release in exchange for forfeiting their fee as volunteers. Nearly all the guards expressed regret at having to finish the experiment early. Whereas the prisoners were beginning to retreat into apathy by the second day, many of the guards quickly showed that they enjoyed the power they had, and began to abuse it. Given that all those involved were volunteers, and had been chosen at random to be guards or prisoners, what does this tell us about the influence of power on human behaviour?

Eysenck and Nias used the laboratory method in their study *Sex, Violence and the Media* (1978). They compare this method with others, and conclude: 'The experimental laboratory method gives the most clear cut and reliable results.'

Experimental effect

But do people behave in laboratories as they do in the real world? Does the knowledge that an experiment is taking place, even if they do not fully understand what it is about, mean that people behave differently from usual? If so, there is a validity problem, in that what is being studied is laboratory behaviour rather than natural behaviour.

This 'experimental effect' is sometimes referred to as the 'Hawthorne Effect'. In 1927, Professor Elton Mayo of Harvard University designed an experiment about the relationship between working conditions, workers' tiredness, and their productivity. He set up a test area in a factory making telephone relays, with five female volunteers who knew the experiment was taking place. Working conditions were matched with those in the main work area, and Mayo then varied such things as room temperature, humidity, hours of work, and rest-breaks. Observation in the first few months showed that, almost regardless of what changes were made, output went up, even when conditions were apparently worsened.

Five hypotheses were suggested to explain this, and each was tested. The most convincing turned out to be that the girls were responding to being involved in the experiment, and were developing strong group loyalties and a wish to please the experimenters. It was the fact of the experiment that was the important independent variable, not the ones that Mayo was working with.

There may also be 'experimenter effect'. This refers to the way in which a particular experimenter may influence different subjects, or to the effect that different experimenters may have on the same subject. These must influence the outcome of the experiment.

47

Field experiments

Partly in response to such criticisms, some researchers have conducted 'field experiments'. These take place in the real world and those involved do not know that an experiment is being conducted.

An example is the experiment conducted by Rosenhan and his colleagues (Rosenhan 1973). They wished to study mental illness and how its symptoms were recognized by medical specialists. They each presented themselves as voluntary patients to mental hospitals, complaining that they were hearing voices. Each was admitted as suffering from schizophrenic symptoms. Once they had been admitted, every volunteer behaved within the mental hospital as normally as they could in the circumstances, and said no more about hearing voices. Their initial interest was in how long it would take before they were caught out, or discharged as cured. In fact, none was ever caught, and none was discharged as cured. Instead, after varying lengths of time, they were discharged as being 'in remission', i.e. their schizophrenia was thought to be still present, but not actually revealing itself in their behaviour. Rosenhan concludes that the diagnosis of mental illness has less to do with the symptoms that are exhibited by patients, and more to do with the way that behaviour is interpreted by doctors who 'know' that someone is mentally ill.

In another experiment, Sissons (1970) arranged for an actor to dress up in a suit and bowler hat and stand on Paddington station, periodically asking people the way to Hyde Park. The same actor then changed into the clothes of a labourer and asked people the same question, with the same wording. Sissons studied the different reactions of those questions. Any systematic variation must have been the result of the reaction of passers-by to the apparent social class of the person they were talking to, since all other variables were held constant.

The further we move away from the laboratory method, the further we are moving from the true experiment, and the closer to what sociologists refer to as the 'comparative method' of social analysis, which will be described in the next section.

Some of these 'field experiments' may be a satisfactory response to the criticisms levelled at laboratory experiments, but they have other problems of their own. The major one is that there is no way that the researcher can hope to be aware of, still less control, all the possible independent variables, and this casts doubt on any conclusions that may be drawn about causes.

The problem works both ways. If we are to control all variables, we have to set up a totally artificial situation. If we want the situation to be as realistic as possible, we have to accept that we cannot control all the variables, and can therefore never be sure that the cause and effect relationships we identify are, in fact, correct.

In addition, there is always the problem of ethics. On the one hand, there are many topics that could be experimented on that are barred by ethical considerations. For example, we could not set up an experiment to test the effect on young babies of being left in complete isolation, except for being fed regularly. We have to rely on the occasional incident of this kind occurring naturally, and study that. On the other hand, what are the ethical problems involved in deceiving volunteers, as did Milgram, or hospital doctors, as did Rosenhan, just for the sake of avoiding the problem of their behaving differently because they knew what the experiment was about?

And yet we must not dismiss experiments in social science. They may not be able to give final answers, but they can provide some very important insights.

Ethnomethodology

This very specialized approach is explained on pp. 88–90, but it is mentioned here because it sometimes uses a kind of experiment. The experiments are of the 'what if' variety, i.e. they ask 'what would happen if we did this?', and are not therefore based on hypothetico-deductive logic. You should, however, remember them when considering the experimental method.

Comparative method

Experiments involve comparing what happens in one situation (the control group) with what happens in another (the experimental group). It is clear that the experimental method is of limited use in sociology because of the difficulty of reproducing social situations in the laboratory, largely because of their scale, but also because they involve the passing of time.

It is these problems that have led to sociologists using the comparative method. In fact, this method has been called the 'natural experiment' or sometimes the 'quasi-experiment' ('quasi' means 'as if'). The sociologist collects information about different societies or social contexts as they are found in the real world, and identifies the similarities and differences between them. In other words, instead of setting up situations either in the laboratory or in the field, the researcher studies what is already going on. The method of argument is based on the same underlying logic as the experiment, a logic first spelled out by John Stuart Mill in the nineteenth century.

Many early sociologists, such as Auguste Comte (1798–1857) compared different societies with the intention of showing that all were evolving along a similar path. Comte produced his 'law of the three stages' of societal development which maintained that all societies, past, present and future, necessarily passed through the same three stages of development. This conclusion was based on extensive, though rather selective, studies of the history of a wide range of societies. Marx, too, drew on comparative material in support of his theory of the inevitable march of history from primitive communism, through feudalism and capitalism, to the ultimate stage of post-revolutionary communism.

It was, however, Weber and Durkheim who based their work most firmly on the comparative method. Weber was interested in the reasons for the emergence of capitalism in western Europe. Why did it occur when it did? Other societies had had similar social and economic systems to that of Europe and had not developed capitalism. Weber studied, particularly,

China and India, but also ancient Palestine and some Islamic countries. Despite their similarities, only Europe had developed capitalism. What Weber sought was a factor that was unique to Europe that he could show was logically connected with the emergence of capitalism.

He found it in Protestantism, or at least the Calvinist version of it. Calvinists believed that every person was predestined by God to go to heaven or to hell. Nothing they could do on earth would affect this destiny. However, rather than seeing this as an excuse for living as they pleased, the Calvinists believed that success in work and in trade was a sign that they were one of the elect rather than one of the damned. Needing this reassurance, they were thus encouraged to innovate, to work hard, and to strive to succeed. However, if their efforts were crowned with success in the form of wealth, they could not spend this profit on worldly goods and comforts, since their religion forbade this. Instead, they would reinvest it in their business enterprises, which would then flourish even more. It is this principle of reinvestment and growth that is the basis of capitalism.

Thus Weber claimed to show that Calvinism was the independent variable that was present in Europe and absent in China and India, and was one of the important causes of the appearance of the dependent variable of capitalism. In addition to showing simply that the factors occurred together, Weber was also able to show that there was an understandable connection between the Calvinists' beliefs and their actions. We can imagine that, if we believed what the Calvinists believed, we would have behaved in the same way.

For Durkheim, comparison was the most important method of sociological analysis. He used it in his study of primitive religion, and in his study of the change from what he called mechanical solidarity to organic solidarity. He compared the legal systems of different societies, and showed that they varied according to how many laws were based on the principle of repression, and how many on the principle of restoring the situation to what it had previously been (restitution). He took the ratio between repressive law and restitutive law as an index of the type of solidarity of the society. This enabled him to test his original hypothesis, which was that an increase in work specialization and the division of labour is linked to the change from mechanical to organic solidarity.

However, Durkheim's most famous example of comparative method was his study of the causes of suicide (Durkheim 1897). In doing this research, Durkheim collected the statistics of suicide in the various areas and regions of France, and of other European countries. He calculated these as suicide rates in relation to the size of the population in which they occurred. Having considered and dismissed various other explanations of suicide, Durkheim then showed how these rates varied systematically with the rates of various other social phenomena, such as religious belief, marital status, urban or rural living, military training or the lack of it, and others. With the help of a mass of statistical calculations, all presented in his book, he showed that there were correlations between these different rates, but he had yet to show that these correlations were causal connections and not mere coincidence. This he did by using the concept of 'social integration'. By manipulating the statistics in various ways, holding one factor constant while varying another, he showed that rates of suicide varied according to the extent to which people were integrated into their social group. Over-integration or under-integration could both cause suicide, as could the disintegration of the group itself, leaving the individual rootless and without moral and social support.

More recently, writers interested in social mobility (the movement of individuals and groups up and down the social scale) have studied rates of social mobility in different societies in an attempt to discover its causes, especially in relation to the process of industrialization. Lipset and Bendix (1959), for example, analysed the results of social mobility research that had been carried out in nine different industrialized societies. In particular, they studied mobility across the line between manual and non-manual classes, both upward and downward, and found that rates were very similar for all the societies. In order to explain these similarities, Lipset and Bendix had to find some factor or factors that were common to all the societies. In the end they found five such factors, of which they felt the most important were the increase in the number of high-status jobs in industrial societies, and the increasing importance attached to qualifications rather than family connections when people were being promoted to higher job levels. These factors, together with others they identified, were part of the industrialization process and, they concluded, explained the similarities in rates of vertical social mobility.

Conclusion

The comparative method lies at the root of any sociological research that goes beyond description. While this has been a relatively short section of the book, its importance is greater than its length would suggest. Any sociologist who is trying to identify the causes of social events and behaviour is going to be involved in making comparisons, whether by means of conducting surveys among different groups of people, or by conducting experiments with control and experimental groups, or by the comparative methods described above. It is fundamental to causal explanation that comparisons are made between instances where the thing to be explained is present and instances where it is absent.

4

Ethnography

'Ethnography' means simply 'writing about a way of life'. This style of research is also referred to as 'field study' or even 'fieldwork' but, since this can sometimes be confused with survey-type research, which may also involve going out into 'the field', this book will use the term 'ethnography'.

At its simplest, ethnography involves the researcher in describing the way of life of a group of people. Such a group may be large, as in the case of community studies of whole towns, or quite small, as in the various studies that have been made of street-corner boys, groups of school-pupils, or people in institutions such as colleges or mental hospitals. The first part of this chapter will concentrate on studies of relatively small groups.

The purpose of such research is to describe the culture and life style of the group of people being studied in a way that is as faithful as possible to the way they see it themselves. The idea is not so much to seek causes and explanations, as is often the case with survey-style research, but rather to 'tell it like it is'. It may well be that, as a result of such descriptions, the researcher, or other people, develop theories about why the people concerned behave as they do. However, such hypotheses are expected to emerge from the research as it goes along, rather than be developed from the start and used as a guide to the kind of data that is sought and collected.

Charles Booth, in his study of the poor, provides one of the earliest justifications of this kind of research:

'It is not easy for any outsider to gain a sufficient insight into the lives of these people. The descriptions of them in the books we read are for the most part as unlike the truth as are the descriptions of aristocratic life in the books they read. Those who know, think it a matter without interest, so that again and again in my enquiries, when some touch of colour has been given illuminating the ways of life among the people who are above the need for help, it has been cut short by a semi-apology: "But that is not what you want to know about" .... Of personal knowledge I have not much .... Yet such as it is, what I have witnessed has been enough to throw a strong light on the materials I have used, and, for me, has made the dry bones live. For three separate periods I have taken up quarters, each time for several weeks, where I was not known, and as a lodger have shared the lives of people .... I became intimately acquainted with some of those I met, and the lives and habits of many others naturally came under observation. My object, which I trust was a fair one, was never suspected, my position never questioned. The people with whom I lived became, and are still, my friends.'

(Booth, in Keating 1976)

The anthropologists

The origins of modern ethnography are to be found in the late nineteenth century, when men like Boas and Rivers studied the ways of life of a variety of tribes by then included in the British Empire. These men were aware of the importance of recognizing that these so-called 'primitive peoples' had complex and elaborate cultures which could be destroyed by the supposedly civilizing influences of the European powers. They did not go so far as to learn the language of the peoples they studied, but they did spell out for later writers the ground rules of such research.

Their influence is apparent in the work of the anthropologists who were working in the period between the two world wars. As the European empires entered their final phase, so anthropologists like D. T. Evans-Pritchard, Bronislaw Malinowski, A. R. Radcliffe-Brown, and the American Margaret Mead (1901–78) made their classic studies of some of the simple societies of the western Pacific and Melanesia, and of certain African tribes. Malinowski is usually regarded as the greatest of these researchers, at least as far as his methods are concerned. In order to see things as the Trobrianders saw them, he joined their communities, learned their language, and lived among them as a member, noting and recording his observations in preparation for writing about them later:

'The anthropologist must relinquish his comfortable position in the long chair on the verandah of the missionary compound, Government station, or planter's bungalow, where, armed with pencil and notebook and at times with a whisky and soda, he has been accustomed to collect statements from informants, write down stories, and fill out sheets of paper with savage texts. He must go out into the villages, and see the natives at work in the gardens, on the beach, in the jungle .... Information must come to him full-flavoured from his own observations of native life, and not be squeezed out of reluctant informants as a trickle of talk. Field work can be done first or second hand even among the savages, in the middle of pile dwellings, not far from actual cannibalism and head-hunting. Open-air anthropology, as opposed to hearsay note-taking, is hard work, but it is also great fun. Only such anthropology can give us the all-round vision of primitive man and primitive culture.'   (Malinowski, quoted in Polsky 1967)

Evans-Pritchard, too, followed this style of research because no other would have enabled him to gain the insights that he wanted. He went to live among the Nuer of the southern Sudan as a vulnerable outsider, relying on their goodwill and friendship to enable him gradually to merge into the background of their everyday lives. As he himself said, it would be pointless to study such peoples with a questionnaire, since they do not write, and, while he certainly gained a great deal of essential information from conversation and discussion, it would have been quite futile to try to conduct any kind of interview until he had gained their trust and confidence, and until he had some idea of what kinds of questions he should be asking.

Margaret Mead's major interest was the way in which adolescence, and gender roles, are differently understood and interpreted in different cultures. She argued that, if she could show that what was regarded as normal behaviour in the United States in fact varies from one society to another, then it followed that such behaviour could not be the result of people's biological characteristics but rather of their culture. She showed, for example, that the behaviour of men and women varied very much among three tribes of New Guinea. Among the Arapesh, both men and women behaved in ways that western society might consider to be 'naturally' female. Among the Mundugamore, both sexes behaved in ways usually associated in our society with aggressive masculinity, and among the Tchambuli the 'normal' male-female roles seemed to be at least partly reversed (Mead 1935). Mead, like Malinowski, went to live among the peoples she was studying, observed their behaviour as a participant in the society, and combined this with some informal interviewing of members of the tribes that she studied closely.

We do have to be a little careful now of the evidence which Mead cited in support of her claim that both gender and adolescence are so culturally varied that they simply cannot be biologically determined. Freeman (1984) has suggested that some of her research was not as thorough as it should have been if she was to make such claims, and even that her desire to reach the conclusions that she did made her see things as she wished to see them, rather than as they actually were. It is her methods, and those of the other anthropologists mentioned, that are our major interest here, but this problem does highlight, at an early stage, one of the basic drawbacks of ethnography —the impossibility of ever checking on the findings of such research by repeating it.

Participant observation

I have referred to Mead's observing her tribes while participating in their everyday lives. 'Participant observation' has always been the central method of ethnographers. It is often combined with data from other sources, especially informal or unstructured interviewing. In fact, the phrase 'participant observation' is sometimes used instead of 'ethnography' or 'fieldwork', but this is misleading. Participant observation is just one method of collecting data, not a complete strategy for social research.

Anthropologists have continued to employ participant observation as their major method of data collection up to the present day but, from about the 1930s onwards, sociology and anthropology grew further and further apart. Sociologists concentrated their attention on complex industrial societies, and anthropologists continued to study simple societies. Recently, there has been a moving together again, but in the 1930s there developed at the University of Chicago a tradition of social research that is now known as the 'Chicago School'. Led by Robert E. Park, this group of researchers, as we saw in chapter 1, devoted their research efforts to detailed studies of their own city. Park specifically recommended that his team followed the methods pioneered by the anthropologists:

'Go and sit in the lounges of the luxury hotels and on the doorsteps of the flophouses; sit on the Gold Coast settees and on the slum shakedowns; sit in Orchestra Hall and in the Star and Garter Burlesk. In short, gentlemen, go get the seats of your pants dirty in *real* research.'

(Park, quoted in Gomm and McNeill 1982)

The Chicago School employed ethnographic methods of data collection, and produced accounts of the lives of a wide variety of social groups, though with an emphasis on the poor and the deviant. They concentrated on observation of people in their 'natural habitat', watching, listening, talking, taking life-histories, and recording.

The pupils of this generation of sociologists are people like Howard Becker and Erving Goffman, and it was their work in the 1960s that gave a new lease of life to ethnographic research after it had fallen into some disuse, in British sociology at least, in the 1950s. The most important characteristic of their work is that it is 'naturalistic'. This means that the account given is rooted in the natural setting of what is being described, and is thus very different from both the formal interview and laboratory research, which involve creating an artificial situation in which the data is collected. David Matza, for example, argues that the exclusive use of questionnaires and formal interviews means that the young delinquent is never studied in his own natural setting, where his behaviour is natural and unselfconscious. Responses to an interview conducted by a stranger, however relaxed and friendly, can never provide a valid picture of the way of life of the subject of the interview. The central characteristic of social action is that it has meaning for the people who are involved in it. They understand what is going on in ways that make sense to them and, if we want to understand their behaviour, and perhaps to explain it, we have to start from where they are. People are active, conscious, and choose to behave as they do, rather than being driven to it by social forces outside their control. Their behaviour may seem inexplicable, and even offensive, to outsiders, but to them it is appropriate to the situation as they themselves see it. It is the researcher's task to 'get inside their heads' until it is possible to see their world as they do. This cannot be achieved through a structured interview or a questionnaire. Theories and explanations must emerge from the work as it goes along.

The phases of ethnographic research

The stages of ethnographic research are even less distinct from each other than those of the survey, but certain phases can be identified.

Choice of topic

As with all research, the first decision to be made is the choice of topic and group to be studied. This choice will always be made as a result of the wider interests of the researcher, and there is the usual interplay here between theoretical assumptions, areas of research interest, and research method chosen (see p. 117).

Deviant behaviour has always been a popular topic for ethnographic research. Given the essentially secret nature of much deviant behaviour, those involved are unlikely to be willing to be interviewed, or at least to give truthful answers, in a survey. In the case of criminals, much early research was based on surveys of those who had been caught and convicted. The problem is that they are a small sample of all criminals, and almost certainly unrepresentative. Clearly, if one is interested in deviant groups, and is convinced that the way to understanding their behaviour is to see the world from their point of view, the best way to achieve this is by near-total immersion in their way of life.

Groups of people who feel under threat are unlikely to respond enthusiastically to a researcher with a questionnaire. Okely (1983), in her study of traveller-gypsies, was at first under pressure from her employers to produce a 'document with a format considered likely to influence the minds of administrators and policy-makers. Greater credence was given to quantitative data, judged "representative", to be obtained by a questionnaire administered to a large number of gypsies.' In practice, she quickly found, as she had known she would, that the method was hopelessly inappropriate for this particular study. 'The gypsies proved brilliantly inconsistent. It was recognized that their answers could not be "coded".' She soon switched to more anthropological methods.

Benson made an ethnographic study of interracial families in Brixton, London. Even without using a questionnaire, she found that:

> 'Research, in the context of Brixton, was at best irrelevant and at worst a tool in the hands of the enemy ... the enemy, of course, varying with the personal perspective of the speaker .... Black people in particular were wary of the motives and activities of whites who wished to know more about them.'
> (Benson 1981)

This still leaves the problem of which particular deviant group to join, and of how typical that group is of all such groups. In practice, ethnographers tend rather to play down the question of whether their particular group is typical of others, but the reader must recognize that the choice of group is a kind of sampling, and the question of representativeness must arise.

Selection of a topic and group is also affected by the fact that some groups have the power to refuse access to researchers. It is no surprise, therefore, that we have no ethnographic studies of powerful decision-making groups, in business or in politics, and many studies of relatively powerless groups. Some groups may, of course, be unconcerned. But have school pupils, or patients in a mental hospital, ever been asked if they agree to having a researcher about the place? The authorities may be asked, but that is a different matter.

Joining the group

Having chosen what group or institution is to be studied, the researcher has to decide what their 'cover story' is going to be. Are they going to tell the people that they are studying them, and be 'overt' about their role as researcher, or are they going to act a part, conduct 'covert' research, and never let on what they are doing? Most researchers start from the assumption that it is morally wrong to conduct research on people who do

61

not know that they are being studied, and will therefore tell them at least that they are writing a book, even if they are not wholly frank about what the book is going to be about. But in some cases the group's behaviour will be disrupted by the presence of a known researcher, and it is in these instances that covert research is conducted. The most obvious examples are studies of groups involved in criminal or at least highly deviant activity. When Humphreys was making his study of homosexual activity in public lavatories in the USA, there was no way in which he could have simply stood around watching what was going on. Nor, however, did he want to be an active participant. He resolved the problem by adopting the role of lookout, warning the men when strangers, particularly police, were approaching. This was a recognized role among the men involved, and Humphreys was accepted as a normal part of this activity. He was, however, arrested on one occasion and, on another, found himself one of a group of men being attacked in a lavatory by a crowd of youths (Humphreys 1970).

Ditton made a study of pilfering among bread roundsmen. He became particularly interested in how they managed to combine this well-organized and criminal activity with an image of themselves as law-abiding citizens. Having worked at a bakery during his university vacations, Ditton had no difficulty in being taken on again. He started out by conducting a questionnaire-based survey, but this soon became a 'blind' to conceal the work he was actually doing in studying pilferage. 'I was partially open ... although I never fully declared that I was chiefly interested in fiddling' (Ditton 1977).

Festinger and his colleagues wished to study what happened in a religious sect when their prophecy that the world was coming to an end on a particular day turned out to be wrong (Festinger, Rieken, and Schachter 1956). In order to do this they traced, via a newspaper report, a certain Mrs Keech, who had prophesied that a flood would cover the earth's surface from the Arctic Circle to the Gulf of Mexico, but that the faithful would be saved by a flying saucer at midnight on the

62

day of the flood, 21 December. Several researchers joined the group, masquerading as believers, and were thus present when midnight came and went without the prophecy being fulfilled. To discover what happened you should look at the book yourself, but, for the moment, consider the ethics of what Festinger and his colleagues did. Were they morally justified in lying to Mrs Keech and her followers and maintaining this lie for several months on end? Certainly, they could not have studied the group if they had been honest about themselves, but perhaps that just means that there are some social contexts that we cannot study. What would be the moral standing of a covert participant observation study of Death Row?

Polsky is very clear about this. He is emphatic that the researcher, when studying criminal groups, should be completely open about what he is doing. This is both because of the moral principle involved, and because, as Polsky believes, the researcher will be spotted by the criminal group in a very short time, and will then be in trouble. He maintains that group members will soon accept the non-criminal character of this new member of their group, and they will behave as they do when he is not among them (Polsky 1967).

Whether the researcher's role is going to be covert or overt, the next problem is to gain access to the group being studied. There have been as many ways of doing this as there have been ethnographic studies done.

Liebow, in his study of a group of black Americans in Washington, describes this crucial first phase of his research. He achieved little on the first day that he spent 'in the field' but on the second day he got into conversation with a group of men about a puppy that one was carrying. Thus he met Tally Jackson, who was to give his name to the book that Liebow finally wrote, *Tally's Corner*:

> 'For more than four hours Tally and I lounged around in the carry-out, talking, drinking coffee, watching people come and go, watching other hangers-on as they bantered with the waitresses, horsed around among themselves, or danced to

the juke-box. Everyone knew Tally and some frequently sought out his attention. Tally sometimes participated in the banter but we were generally left undisturbed when we were talking. When I left at two o'clock, Tally and I were addressing each other by first names ("Elliot" was strange to him and we settled for "Ellix") and I was able to address the two waitresses by their first names without feeling uncomfortable. I had also learned to identify several other men by their names or nicknames, had gotten hints on personal relationships, and had a biographical sketch (part of it untrue I learned later) of Tally.'   (Liebow 1967)

Liebow's success was the greater since he was a white man and Tally and his friends were black.

Some researchers have been able to make use of their own skills to gain access to a group. Becker's expertise as a jazz pianist made possible his study of dance musicians (Becker 1963). Polsky used his ability at the pool-table in his study of 'hustlers':

'My study of pool-room hustling extended over eight months in 1962 and 1963. It proceeded by a combination of: (a) direct observation of hustlers as they hustled; (b) informal talks, sometimes hours long, with hustlers; (c) participant observation – as hustler's opponent, hustler's backer, and as hustler. Since methods (b) and (c) drew heavily on my personal involvement with the pool-room world, indeed are inseparable from it, I summarize aspects of that involvement below.

Billiard playing is my chief recreation. I have frequented pool-rooms for over twenty years, and at one pool-room game, three-cushion billiards, am considered a far better than average player.'   (Polsky 1967)

When a researcher is investigating an institution of some kind, it is usually necessary to get permission from the authorities for the work to be done. Thus Lacey (1970), in his study of a secondary school, had to obtain permission from the chief education officer and the headmaster before he entered the school. But this must raise the question of the effect of the researcher on the researched. If the researcher is seen as connected with the authority structures of the institution, will this not have some effect on the behaviour of those being observed? Lacey does not discuss this, but Dalton has firm views in his study of industrial managers:

'In no case did I make a formal approach to the top management of any of the firms to get approval or support for the research. Several times I have seen other researchers do this and have watched higher managers set the scene and limit the enquiry to specific areas – outside management proper – as though the problem existed in a vacuum.'

(Dalton 1959)

Corrigan felt it was important, in his study of the boys in an urban secondary school, to create a role for himself which was not threatening to them:

'This was equally true of the teachers, since they, together with the headmaster, could have decided to stop my research whenever they felt it threaten them; equally, if they had accepted me with open arms it would have meant that the boys would not have trusted me greatly.'

(Corrigan 1979)

In the end, he adopted the role of 'cockney writer', a role which was genuine, and which showed the boys that Corrigan was interested in them for themselves.

Further reading

Obtain a copy of Hargreaves (1967). Read Appendix One. What effect do you think the presence of a participant observer would have on your classroom?

Having once gained access to the group or institution being studied, the researcher enters the first phase of the research proper. In this he or she follows very broad lines of action, trying to be as open-minded and receptive as possible, seeing all the patterns that begin to emerge. The researcher is little different from anyone else joining a new group and trying to be accepted by them. We are all able, at a common-sense level, to identify what is acceptable behaviour in any new group. What makes the researcher different is that the purpose of making these observations is not only to become a member of the group but also to write an account of its way of life. To do this, the researcher has to remain detached from the group at the same time as becoming a member of it. This is the key to successful ethnographic research. Researchers have to monitor not only the actions and behaviour of the group members, but also their own activities, and they must cultivate self-criticism and self-awareness. The trick is to see the social context as the regular participants do, while at the same time remaining a detached observer of events.

All researchers agree that it is important to remain inconspicuous at this stage. As Polsky (1967) says: 'Initially, keep your eyes and your ears open, but keep your mouth shut.' Whyte (1955) agrees: 'As I sat and listened, I learned the answers to questions I would not have had the sense to ask if I had been getting my information solely on an interviewing basis.'

The other most obvious difference between the researcher and the ordinary new member of a social group is that the former must keep detailed and accurate notes and records of everything observed and every impression gained. This can be done in a variety of ways, but researchers are unanimous that it is essential to write up the events of a day before going to bed at night, or, at the very latest, the following morning. This entails taking notes wherever possible, without being too obvious about it. Ditton, who started by using the lavatory as a place to make notes secretly, took his first notes on lavatory paper. Gans tried not to act like a formal researcher:

'(I) rarely took notes during the thousands of informal conversational interviews. Instead I memorized the answers, made quick notes as soon as I could, and later wrote the whole interview in my field diary. (Although a famous novelist has recently garnered considerable publicity for memorizing his interviews, this has long been standard practice for many sociologists.)' (Gans 1967)

Clearly, to take notes obviously and constantly is sure to affect the behaviour of a group, and there is no question of the covert researcher being able to do this. But is it really possible for researchers to remember details of conversations as they claim to do? Or all the details of complex and perhaps fast-moving events? Many researchers are surprised and delighted at their ability to remember conversations almost word for word. Pryce had to rely heavily on memory:

'My method was to write down these observations as soon as possible after hearing or observing them. The rule of thumb I constantly exercised was to record them while they were still fresh in my mind, generally the same day. It was my practice never to record anything, especially conversations, after three days ... it is surprising how efficient one's memory can become with practice.' (Pryce 1979)

In any case, it must be recognized that these notes, however full and detailed, are a selection from all the events that the researcher witnessed, and that this selection is made on the basis of what the researcher considers to be significant. This in turn means that there is sampling involved, and it is sampling based on the judgement of the researcher. As with the survey, the researcher's judgement about what is important must affect the outcome of the research.

Middle phase of research

As the research progresses, so ideas start to crystallize. The researcher begins to build relationships with people, and certain individuals emerge as 'key informants' for the research. The 'key informant' will often be the same individual as made possible the researcher's access to the group, and may become almost a partner in the research. The most famous of these figures, 'Doc' in *Street Corner Society* (Whyte 1955), certainly became an assistant to Bill Whyte, and indeed gave Whyte another ethical problem, as both he and Doc came to see that Doc's behaviour had changed as a result of Whyte's work. Doc said:

'You've slowed me down plenty since you've been here. Now, when I do something, I have to think what Bill Whyte would want to know about it and how can I explain it. Before I used to do things by instinct.'   (Whyte 1955)

Tally, of *Tally's Corner*, is another key informant, and Liebow (1967) acknowledges that this may mean that the account given in the book is more that of Tally himself than of others who lived around the street corner. How might the book have been different if Liebow had met someone else on that day at the 'carry-out'?

The researcher will begin to penetrate the 'fronts' that are always put up for an outsider, and will work towards developing a true and authentic understanding of the setting.

Towards the end of this phase, the researcher may be able to start conducting interviews with some of the people being studied, provided of course that his role is overt. Such interviews will be unstructured, and are sometimes called 'guided conversations'. In a normal conversation, the people involved are of equal status, and any one of them can change the topic under discussion or introduce new points. In the guided conversation, the researcher has more of this power; he will ensure that the topics that have emerged as important are discussed, and will make notes, or even a recording, of the respondent's answers. Becker *et al.* (1961) conducted such interviews at the end of the second year of their research with medical students, using a schedule organized around material gathered from participant observation. They even used phrases originally employed by the students themselves in informal conversation. They noted a 'marked difference between what we observed students doing while they were in school and the way they talked about school in retrospect' (see p. 29).

Final phase of research

In the last phase of the research, the researcher will be in a position to begin to test ideas about what is going on and to identify patterns of behaviour. It is now that the final form of the book begins to emerge, and the researcher has to begin to withdraw from the research group.

This stage includes the publication of the research report. The people who have been studied will probably be interested in what is said about them, and this may affect what the researcher writes. Whatever promises of anonymity are given, the people involved will recognize themselves in the characters portrayed, and this may cause difficulties. If criminal activities are clearly involved, then the researcher has an ethical problem. Parker faced this dilemma in his study of a group of adolescent boys on Merseyside:

> 'The major problem in writing up is an ethical one, however. The fieldwork data basically fell into three categories: that which I felt could definitely be published, that which could definitely not be published, and that which I was unsure about. The third category was eventually broken up and distributed into the yes/no compartments through consultation with those involved and colleagues. Becker has pointed out in reviewing studies of this nature that publication will almost inevitably "make somebody angry". This is probably true; my main concern is that no harm comes to The Boys.' (Parker 1974)

Patrick made a study of a Glasgow gang:

> 'I have deliberately allowed some years to pass between the

completion of the fieldwork and publication. The main reasons for the delay have been my interest in self-preservation, my desire to protect the members of the gang, and my fear of exacerbating the gang situation in Glasgow which was receiving nationwide attention in 1968 and 1969. Reasons of personal safety also dictate the use of a pseudonym.'

(Patrick 1973)

Participant observer, participant, or observer?

On reading several of these research reports, it is apparent that the role of the researcher varies from one study to another, and indeed often varies from one stage of the same study to another. One such variation concerns the extent to which the researcher's role is known to the people being studied. Gold (1958) suggests that the researcher may be: (a) a complete participant, concealing his true identity and intentions from the group, and living entirely as they do; or (b) a participant-as-observer, actively involved in the group, but they know the researcher is not really one of them; or (c) an observer-as-participant, a less common mode, usually involving a brief visit with limited participation.

Gans classifies the roles in terms of the actual behaviour of the researcher:

'1 Researcher acts as observer .... physically present at the event which he observes, but does not really participate in it ....

2 Researcher participates, but as researcher .... participation is determined by his research interests, rather than by the roles required in the situation he is studying ....

3 Researcher participates ... the researcher temporarily abdicates his study role and becomes a "real" participant. After the event, his role reverts back to that of an observer – and in this case, an analyst of his own actions while being a real participant.'

(Gans 1962)

This raises the ever-present danger of the researcher's 'going native'. This expression originated with the anthropologists, and refers to the possibility that the researcher will become over-involved with the people being studied, and so lose the detachment that is an essential part of the participant observer's role. Pryce (1979) discusses this difficulty with great honesty.

Another aspect of this problem arises when the researcher has to decide whether to become involved in criminal activity. This is a risk that is always present for covert researchers, such as Patrick (1973) and Ditton (1977). Patrick, in fact, left his group abruptly when the violence became too much for him. Polsky argues that this is the main reason why such research should not be covert. If the people know from the start where the researcher draws the line, then the problem does not arise. Whyte, by contrast, found himself 'personating' at an election. That is, he voted more than once, as was quite common among the people he was studying (Whyte 1955).

Conclusion

The ethnographer's central concern is to provide a description that is faithful to the world-view of the participants in the social context being described. Explanations of social action may emerge from this description, but that is not the primary purpose. The test of its validity is whether the subjects of the research accept it as a true account of their way of life. The researcher must not impose any prior assumptions on the subject matter, and should allow any theory or hypothesis to emerge from what is observed and recorded.

It is in this that the great strength of ethnographic research lies. Behaviour is observed in its natural setting, and it is possible to make a study of social process, rather than being limited to the snapshot or series of snapshots of the survey researcher. The emphasis is on describing the meaning of the situation for those involved in it. What makes the work scientific is the care taken to avoid error, to be thorough and exhaustive, and to check and recheck all findings.

There are, however, several problems with this style of research. It is very laborious and time-consuming, involving the researcher full-time for at least a matter of months, and sometimes years. It is expensive in terms of paying the salary or the research grant of the researcher for this time, while he or she is engaged in no other work.

Critics of ethnography stress its unreliability. There is no way that the research can be repeated as a means of checking its descriptions and conclusions. It is not possible to judge whether the social context studied is in any way typical, or representative. Perhaps the researcher became over-involved in the group studied, and lost the detachment that is fundamental to this method. Perhaps the presence of the researcher changed the behaviour of the group more than was realized. Ethnography necessarily involves a narrow view of the group or institution studied, since the researcher cannot, by definition, study the wider context within which the research setting is located.

Further reading

The style of this research makes it very difficult for the student to get the feel of it through first-hand experience. On the other hand, much of it is very readable. The following studies are all recommended on the grounds that they are clearly written, interesting in their own right, and include discussions of the ethnographic research method:

Becker et al. (1961)   Becker et al. (1968)   Benson (1981)
Corrigan (1979)   Ditton (1977)   Hargreaves (1967)
Humphreys (1970)   Liebow (1967)   Okely (1983)
Parker (1974)   Patrick (1973)   Plant (1975)
Polsky (1967)   Pryce (1979)   Whyte (1955)
Willis (1977)

It is not necessary, though it is desirable, to read the whole book in order to understand the methods used. In all these books, methods are discussed in a separate section.

Even so, there is no chance that any one student will have time to read more than a couple of books. In my group, each student takes one study and prepares a report for the rest, using the guide that appears on pp. 125–29 of this book. In this way, everyone learns something about many books.

If you have time to read only one book, make it Whyte (1955), or the new edition published in 1981.

Griffin (1962) is not sociology, but is nevertheless valuable reading. It is the story of a white man who has his skin chemically darkened so that he can experience what it is like to be black in the southern USA.

Activity

It is easier for students to simulate ethnographic research than a survey. Gomm and McNeill (1982), Item 55, suggests that it is important that this does not become mere story-telling, and makes the following suggestions of contexts that might be studied: a swimming pool; a school playground; nursery schools; queueing behaviour; the football match; underground trains; the holiday beach. Item 60 gives detailed suggestions about making an ethnographic study of a courtroom in session.

Community studies

As we have seen, ethnographic studies aim to describe the way of life of a society or group of people. Where that group is quite small, such as a street gang, the main method of data collection used will be participant observation, perhaps supported by a limited amount of unstructured interviewing.

If, however, the group to be studied is larger, then a wider range of methods will be necessary, and we are dealing with a 'community study'. The tradition of community research can be dated from the work of the Chicago School, which includes the classic studies of Muncie, Indiana, USA, carried out by the Lynds and published as *Middletown* (1929) and *Middletown in Transition* (1937).

Such studies involve a researcher or a team of researchers in studying a whole community of people, usually in a small town or village, or possibly part of a larger town. The method is always for the researcher to go to live in the community being studied, and to become involved with the residents as a participant observer, but the community researcher will also use a wide variety of other sources of data, as is shown here:

'My actual fieldwork employed six major approaches:

1 Use of the West End's facilities. I lived in the area, and used its stores, services, institutions, and other facilities as much as possible. This enabled me to observe my own and other people's behaviour as residents of the area.
2 Attendance at meetings, gatherings, and public places ....
3 Informal visiting with neighbours and friends ....
4 Formal and informal interviewing of community functionaries ....
5 Use of informants. Some of the people I interviewed became informants, who kept me up to date on those phases of West End life with which they were familiar.
6 Observation. I kept my eyes and ears open at all times.'

(Gans 1962)

'While the research was being done the members of the team made their homes in or near Banbury. Participation in the life of the town was a main method of the work. Each research worker took part in a different sphere .... The published records about Banbury were analysed. A pilot questionnaire followed by a schedule enquiry into over 1,000 households was used .... a study was made, by interview of the leading members and analysis of the records, of all the formal organizations of Banbury ....

Kinship was studied by interview of a number of selected families .... In (the) study of neighbours, the focused interview was the main method used .... Information was gained from key informants.'
(Stacey 1960)

The problems of this kind of research are those of all ethnography, but with some special features. The first is gaining access to the community in question. This may be done simply by taking up residence in the area, without saying anything to anyone other than the organization sponsoring the research. This was done by Gans in his study of suburban America (Gans 1967).

By contrast, when Stacey and her colleagues decided to make a restudy of Banbury, they felt that they should ask permission of that town before they did so. But who should be approached? The mayor? The council? The general public via the local paper? In the end: 'A public meeting at which the mayor presided was held in 1948 before the work began. Reports of any major events were published in the local press and occasionally short articles about the work.'

Then there is the question of how many researchers should be used. If there is only one, he or she will never be able to cover all aspects of community life, and may even be disqualified, by reason of age, sex, or colour, from participating in certain activities. Pryce (1979) points out that, as a male, he 'had only limited access to the women for research purposes'. For this reason, some community studies, such as the Banbury restudy (Stacey 1975) have used teams of researchers, taking care to include a variety of social types in their number. The more complex the society being studied, the more specialist groups it is going to have.

What role should the researchers take on? Should they become deeply involved in the community, and risk losing the detachment needed in such work? Or should they remain marginal figures, seen as threatening by nobody, but at the same time, therefore, not really getting to know anyone in depth? In a large community such a marginal role may be

75

possible, and the researcher can move from one group to another without difficulty, but in a small village, or in a small community in a larger town, it is essential that the researcher be 'placed' in some way. Frankenberg (1957), in his study of a small Welsh village, became secretary of the local football team. Other writers have found that the role of 'author' is enough to see them through, especially in communities where such figures are familiar.

Lastly, the researcher has to consider the effects that publication of the book may have on the community portrayed in it, and particularly on any individuals who may feature. Of course, the author will usually give the community a fictitious name, and also change the names of all key informants, but those who know the community concerned, and certainly all those who live in it, will not have much difficulty in identifying who is who. In the case of a large community this may be less significant, but where a small community is described there can be no anonymity for anyone. Is the researcher's responsibility to the people he has studied, or to the people who will read the book? Is it a case of 'publish and be damned' or do certain ethical codes take precedence? Every community will have its secrets, and every individual in it will have views that they would not normally express to others, but do express to the researcher.

Community studies, like all social research, are limited in time. A community is always changing and evolving, and even a year's study (three years in the case of the Banbury study) barely touches on this process. Some studies have, therefore, been repeated some years later, in an attempt to see what changes have taken place. The *Middletown* studies mentioned above are examples of this, and the Banbury study and restudy (Stacey 1960 and 1975) found significant changes had taken place.

The distinction between community studies and small-scale ethnographies is not clear cut. While a study such as Festinger, Rieken, and Schachter's *When Prophecy Fails* (see p. 62) is clearly not a community study, and one like Frankenberg's

Village on the Border clearly is, others, such as Whyte's *Street Corner Society*, fall somewhere between the two. Generally speaking, the wider the variety of data-collection methods used, and the larger the group studied, the more we are dealing with a community study.

The issue is further complicated by work such as Newby's study of farmworkers in East Anglia (Newby 1977), which employs all the methods used by Gans and by Stacey, and yet is more of a survey than a community study. One of the best known of all British sociological studies, Young and Willmott's *Family and Kinship in East London* (1957), could be said to be a community study, though it has a specific focus and is based mainly, though not entirely, on data collected through a social survey.

The point to recognize is, of course, that it is futile to waste time classifying studies into neat little boxes. As stated on p. 12, research studies in the real world often use a variety of methods, chosen for their suitability for the task in hand.

Activity

It is very difficult for a single student to carry out a community study, though a group might take it on as a year's project. There are some ideas in Gomm and McNeill (1982), Item 51.

Further reading

The next best thing is to read about a community study. I recommend Stacey's two books (1960 and 1975), and those by Gans (1962 and 1967). The latter have more humour. Bell and Newby (1971) has a very good chapter on community study as a method, and many summaries of studies done in Britain and America. From these, you will be able to decide which ones to read for yourself. Exactly the same applies to Frankenberg (1966), which is limited to communities in Britain.

5

Other research methods

There are many other ways of doing sociological research. Some are very specialized, and are unlikely to concern the readers of this book at this stage of their studies, but several will be introduced now, albeit briefly.

Longitudinal studies

One of the problems of sociological research, especially survey-style research, is that it is a snapshot of the social context which it is studying. It is, therefore, difficult to provide a sense of history or of social change. The longitudinal study, sometimes known as a 'panel study', is an attempt to respond to this problem.

The usual procedure is for a sample, which may be referred to as the 'panel', to be selected in the usual way, as described on pp. 32–5 above, and for data about this sample to be collected at regular intervals over a period of years. The best way to show what this involves is by examples.

In 1946, under the supervision of the Population Investigation Committee, a survey was conducted of the experience of every mother who had borne a child in the first week in March of that year. The results were published as *Maternity in Great Britain* in 1948. It had not originally been intended to carry on the research after that date, but it was so successful that funding was obtained to set up a panel study. A sample of 5,362 of the original children was then drawn. By 1950, 4,688 of the parents were still available to the research team, and another survey was conducted, the results of which were published in 1958 as *Children Under Five*, which concentrated particularly on the health of the children.

The best known (to sociologists) of the surveys conducted with this sample was published as *The Home and the School*, by J. W. B. Douglas, in 1964; 4,195 of the children were found still to be living in England and Wales, and 3,418 of these (81.5 per cent) were tested for various aspects of intelligence at the ages of eight and eleven. The results of these tests were correlated with details of the children's home backgrounds.

By 1962, when the children were in their sixteenth year, the number still resident in Great Britain was 4,720, of whom 3,626 (76.8 per cent) were given further tests. The resulting account of their experience in secondary school was published with the title *All Our Future* (Douglas 1968).

While this longitudinal study is one of the most famous, it is by no means the only one. The National Child Development Study has been following the development of all the children born in Britain in the week 3–9 March, 1958. Their first major report was *11,000 Seven Year Olds* published in 1966. A study of the health, education, and home environment of the children was published in 1972, and attracted a good deal of attention: *From Birth to Seven* by R. Davie and his colleagues.

Another more recent example of this approach is the work of the Child Health and Education Survey. This is a study of children born in the second week of April, 1970. Over 16,550 were born, and 13,135 were traced and studied in 1975.

The most striking finding is the enormous range of social and economic circumstances in which children are brought up (Osborn, Butler, and Morris 1984).

Lastly we can refer again to the work of the Newsons in Nottingham. In their first study, they drew a sample of 773 babies born in Nottingham in the early 1960s. The mothers of 709 of these babies were successfully interviewed within two weeks of the baby's first birthday, and the findings published (Newson and Newson 1963). With the success of that first book, the Newsons were able to obtain funds for follow-up studies, but had by then lost contact with many of their original sample. For their second book, they interviewed 700 mothers of four-year-old children, but only 275 of these were from the original sample (Newson and Newson 1968). Thereafter, their books have been follow-up studies of this second group of children.

The advantages of longitudinal studies are that they make it possible to study change over time, though as a series of snapshots rather than as a continuous process. In this respect they are similar to ethnographic restudies (p. 76).

There are several difficulties with longitudinal studies, in addition to the usual problems of sample-based survey research. First, it may be difficult to recruit a sample of people who know that they are taking on a very long-term commitment. Generally, people are rather flattered at the thought of being so important, but this may in turn create the problem that they become untypical because they know that they are in the sample, and will be questioned regularly about their lives, activities, and attitudes.

Then there is the problem of keeping in touch with the sample. Members will die, move away, emigrate, and perhaps change their minds about continuing with the work. Small children may have no choice about being included, but could develop strong feelings about it as they grow up. We have seen how the 1946 sample decreased with the passing of time, and this must raise questions about its continuing representativeness. Are those who drop out, for whatever reason, untypical of the whole group? It may be possible to recruit new members to the panel, as did the Newsons, but this raises further questions.

The research team also needs to be held together. Work like this requires continuing enthusiasm of a kind that may not outlast the departure of the original members, and their replacement with new people. The continuous presence of Douglas in the studies of the 1946 sample has been important to the success of that work.

Lastly there is the question of cost, always important with social research, and particularly so here. Most funding agencies are, understandably, unwilling to take on a commitment to pay for research over a period of perhaps twenty years or more. Most of these studies have had a struggle to remain solvent, and have depended on the generosity of charitable foundations such as Nuffield and Ford, as well as finance from government agencies, often via the health services. In addition, they have made use of health visitors and others as free interviewers.

Before leaving the topic of longitudinal studies, it is worth pointing out that the Census can be seen as an example. Carried out every ten years since 1801, with the exception of 1941, it has most of the characteristics of the longitudinal survey except, of course, that it is a study of the whole population rather than a sample. It is not possible to use the Census to follow a particular group of people through their lives, but it is perfectly feasible to study the changing population structure of, say, a particular district. It is invaluable to the sociologist who wishes to trace broad patterns of social change, and to make comparisons between the social conditions of one period and another (see also p. 93).

Mass Observation

This is the name of an organization founded in Britain in 1937. It was influenced by the traditions of anthropology, and Malinowski played an important role in its early development.

Its object was 'observation by everyone of everyone, including themselves'.

Mass Observation's work was carried out through a combination of many methods. Interviewing was done both directly and indirectly, via what amounted to eavesdropping; there was participant and non-participant observation; auto-biographical statements and life-histories were recorded, as were notes, diaries, and other documents. Informants were a mixture of a national panel of part-time volunteers, and a small team of full-time researchers who went to live in the areas they studied, such as 'Worktown', a Lancashire cotton town, and 'Metrop', a London borough. At one time, over a thousand diaries were being kept, but after the war the methods became more survey-based and Mass Observation Ltd became a conventional market research company. The emphasis remained always on the lives of 'ordinary' people. The reports of Mass Observation are full of down-to-earth quotations about ordinary matters of concern in people's everyday lives.

Observation

We are already familiar with participant observation, but some sociological research has been carried out by observation alone. The main reason for this is to reduce or eliminate the risk that people will be affected by the presence of a new member of their social group. This can only be achieved fully when the observation is carried out without the knowledge of the observed, such as through one-way glass, or in circumstances where the observer is 'lost in the crowd'. If the observer is visibly present, even though not participating, there is still the suspicion that his presence is affecting what is happening.

An example of such work is that of Flanders (1970), who studied interaction in school classrooms. Having sat in on many lessons, he produced a list of ten categories of interaction. The observer's task is then to observe what goes on in a classroom and, every three seconds, to tick the category that best describes what has been happening during that period. This produces a statistical, or 'quantified', account of what is going on, which can then be compared with other lessons and other teachers. A shortened version of Flanders's list of categories is given in *Figure 4*.

Figure 4   Categories for interaction analysis

Teacher talk

Indirect influence	1	Accepts feelings
	2	Praises or encourages
	3	Accepts or uses idea of student
	4	Asks questions
Direct influence	5	Lecturing
	6	Giving directions
	7	Criticizing, or justifying authority

Student talk

	8	Student talk ... response
	9	Student talk ... initiation
	10	Silence or confusion

Source: Flanders (1970)

Activities

1 You could try using this set of categories to conduct observation of your own classroom. You should, however, look at Flanders's explanation of it before you start (Flanders 1970).

2 Draw up a set of categories for some other social activity, such as a family evening at home, or the behaviour of a small group in a school canteen. You will have to think carefully about the intervals at which you 'score' what is happening.

The development of videotape and portable cameras has opened up another whole world of data to sociologists. Making a recording of, for example, people walking along the street, enables the researcher to study the unwritten rules which apply when people are trying to pass each other on a narrow pavement.

83

It is worth stressing that this method of study is useful only to those who are interested in the detail of everyday social life, and whose research overlaps with that of the social psychologist who studies the behaviour of people in small groups.

Time budgeting

In this case, the researcher asks the subjects of the research to keep a detailed diary of their activities during a given period. As Mills explains it, in Young and Willmott (1973):

'The basic information it contains is the duration of activities and their sequence and timing. The fact that it aims to provide a systematic account of time use is what distinguishes it from the literary diary. The time budget .... may record not only the activities themselves but the people with whom they were performed, and the location of activities. There may also be subjective assessments of activities, such as how far they were "routine", or "pleasurable", or how far the respondent would like to do them more or less often ....

The primary advantage of time budgets is their sheer comprehensiveness. They have obvious advantages over ordinary questionnaires and "checklists": with these one can in practice ask only about a limited number of activities which must be precisely specified in advance. Relatively informal activities, such as "napping" and casual encounters, the undergrowth of a person's day, cannot easily be got at by interview.'

Activity

Keep a time-budget diary of your own activities for a twenty-four-hour period. Remember that every moment must be accounted for, and that the description of what you did should be detailed. A description like 'Relaxing' is not clear enough. Do you think the account you produce could be used by a researcher?

The life-history

A 'life-history' or 'life-story' is the autobiography of a person which has been obtained through interview and guided conversation.

The use of the life-history in modern sociology began with the Chicago School of the 1930s, whose work has been described on p. 58. Just as their main interest was in the ways of life of people as seen by the people themselves, so they tried to get a sense of the past into their work by using life-histories. Besides *The Polish Peasant* (see p. 101), the most important early example of this is Shaw's *The Jack-Roller: A Delinquent Boy's Own Story* (1930). In Becker's introduction to later editions of this book, he describes the value of the life-history in sociology. It is not fiction, nor is it conventional autobiography, which tends to say what the author wishes us to know. The sociologist's task, compared with the novelist's, is to make the life-history:

> 'more down to earth, more devoted to our purposes than those of the author, less concerned with artistic values than with a faithful rendering of the subject's experience and interpretation of the world he lives in. The sociologist who gathers a life-history takes steps to ensure that it covers everything we want to know, that no important fact or event is slighted, that what purports to be factual squares with other available evidence and that the subject's interpretations are honestly given.'   (Becker in Shaw 1930)

This approach, like other kinds of ethnography, places most importance on the person's own interpretations and explanations of their behaviour.

What is the value of the life-history? As Becker says, every story can play its part in making up the mosaic that will, in the end, be our picture of the social life of the time and place being studied. We can test the usefulness of wide-ranging theories of juvenile delinquency by reading books like *The Jack-Roller* and seeing if they bear any resemblance to the theory. A life-story can often liven up what has become a very dry and even boring area of social research. It can tell us something very vivid about the life of a type of person whom we may never meet. We can see him or her as a person rather than as a stereotype. The life-history reminds us that we are always talking, in the end, about people, and this makes it a favoured research tool of the ethnographic researcher. Oscar Lewis's studies of poverty (1964, 1968) are an excellent example of this method, in combination with others.

In recent years, the life-history technique has had a revival in sociological research, being used by those who wish to develop 'oral history'. Oral history enables us to take account of those many aspects of history that are not recorded in documents. It puts a whole new perspective on the study of the past, placing the lives of ordinary people at the centre, rather than the activities of monarchs and politicians. Combining life-histories with the use of personal documents such as letters and diaries can show how ordinary people lived in the past.

Oral history does not have to be collected from the very old, though books like Ronald Blythe's *Akenfield* and *The View in Winter* are marvellous examples of such work. Accounts of the 1960s from those who were teenagers then are a vital source of data on youth cultures, as will be the accounts of 1980s teenagers to the students of 2010.

The problems of life-histories and oral history are fairly self-evident: they cannot be shown to be representative or reliable. They are a view of the past from the standpoint of the present, and this raises questions of the accuracy of the recall of facts, and about the interpretive framework through which memories are recalled. The past can only be recalled through the perspective of the present.

Activity

There is great scope for a group research project in oral history. Ideas, advice, and sources of information can be found in Gomm and McNeill (1982).

Case-studies

Social research, to be valuable, does not have to be based on a representative sample. A case-study can be carried out, using almost any method of research, though the less statistical methods are usual.

A case-study involves the detailed study of a single example of whatever it is that the sociologist wishes to investigate. It may prompt further, more wide-ranging research, providing ideas to be followed up later, or it may be that some broad generalization is brought to life by a case-study. There is no claim to representativeness, and the essence of the technique is that each subject studied, whether it be an individual, a group, an event, or an institution, is treated as a unit on its own.

Strike at Pilkingtons by Lane and Roberts (1971) is an account of an industrial dispute at one large firm in Britain. It tells the story of what happened, 'examining the strike from the points of view of each of its major groups of participants'. Lane and Roberts conducted a survey of attitudes and opinions among the strikers, observed the activities of the strike committee, and had lengthy interviews with management, shop stewards, and strikers. One of the authors lived in St Helens for the last three weeks of the strike, becoming as immersed as possible in all aspects of the activities of the strike committee. They collected documents and used press reports. Lane and Roberts do not claim that the strike was typical of other strikes. What they do maintain is that a vividly told story can make an important contribution to our knowledge of how and why strikes occur.

The Rapoports (1971), in their study of married couples who both have a professional career, chose to investigate just five such couples by means of extended in-depth interviews, rather than attempting a survey.

In a sense, any ethnographic study is a case-study, since all such research concentrates on a relatively small group or a single institution. However, many claim that they are typical of others, while a case-study does not usually make this claim. It is somewhere on the borders between social research and journalism.

Ethnomethodology

Two preliminary points should be made about what is sometimes regarded as a very obscure area of sociology. The first is that its obscurity is caused more by the way in which ethnomethodologists express themselves than by the actual complexity of their ideas, which are based, fundamentally, on a very simple argument. The second point is that ethnomethodology is exactly what its name suggests. It is the study of the ways in which people create and construct their way of life. It is not a theory, or a perspective, but rather a way of analysing everyday life according to a particular set of assumptions. Accordingly, it is appropriate to say a few words about it as a method, though the reader who wishes to explore it further should read the relevant chapter in *Perspectives in Sociology*, edited by Cuff and Payne (1984).

The central idea of ethnomethodology is that the orderliness of social life is not the result of people obeying social norms or giving way to social pressures, but rather that orderliness is attained by all those involved working to achieve it. The orderliness is produced by the participants, on every occasion that they interact. For Garfinkel, the founder of ethnomethodology, social events are entirely the product of the actions of those 'members' involved at any particular moment. People perceive the world as though it were guiding and constraining them. Garfinkel's interest is not in whether they are right or wrong in perceiving it in this way, but rather in how they come to perceive it in this way, and what effect this perception has on their actions. People need to make enough sense of any social event to be able to act appropriately. Garfinkel's recommendation to sociologists is:

> 'Look around you and everywhere you will find ordinary persons going about their everyday business performing familiar, unremarkable activities. This mundane fact is the very crux of the social world. The ability of members successfully to perform practical activities in collaboration with others is what makes the social world possible.

Therefore, take these practical actions and examine them for how they are accomplished. You will find that the methods involved are complex and sophisticated, yet they are possessed (and require to be possessed) by pretty nearly everyone.'   (Cuff and Payne 1984)

Ethnomethodology has developed various ways of demonstrating these unwritten rules of social life, and of showing how they are continuously achieved by social actors. There is the disruptive experiment, invented by Garfinkel himself. In this, the ethnomethodologist deliberately disrupts the taken-for-granted routine of social life, and watches what happens. One famous example of this was when he asked students to pretend that they were boarders in their own homes, and to behave accordingly. That is to say, they were more formal, more polite, and rather more distant than usual, asking permission to do things that usually they would have done without question. The effect on others in the home highlighted, for Garfinkel, the taken-for-granted rules of family life, which became apparent when they were broken rather than when they were being achieved and observed. The taken-for-granted world was shown as the fragile construction that it really is.

Another strand of ethnomethodology is conversational analysis. Given that social order is continuously worked at and achieved by members, the question arises, 'How is this done?' What is the main method that people use to achieve social order? The answer is 'conversation and talk', and this led ethnomethodologists like Harvey Sacks into detailed analysis of conversation as a practical accomplishment of ordinary people. His aim is to show what are the taken-for-granted rules of conversation and how we describe the world to one another so that we all make sense of it in similar ways. As a result, we are able to interact with each other. He is particularly interested in the way that words and sentences change their meaning according to the context in which they are said and heard, and in the ways in which we all fill in the unspoken background of what is said to us. To understand the meaning of what is said to us is a cultural accomplishment that we take for granted. The ethnomethodologist does not take it for granted. He tries to spell out how we do it.

Schegloff has made studies of the rules of conversation in so far as they govern who speaks when, and how we know when it is our turn to speak. For example, what are the rules that govern the opening of a telephone conversation? And how do we end the conversation in such a way that both persons involved recognize that the end has been reached, and neither feels snubbed? Of course, sometimes we do feel that the other person has been rather abrupt in ending the conversation, and that is the moment when we should do our ethnomethodological analysis to identify what it was that they, or we, failed to do as part of bringing the conversation to a proper and recognizable end. If we can identify it, then we have identified a taken-for-granted rule of everyday life.

Lastly, ethnomethodologists have made studies of what they call 'practical reasoning'. How do people arrive at conclusions about what is going on in a particular instance? This process is not only one that occurs in everyday life, but has also to be carried out by scientists in the laboratory, or by coroners in coroners' courts (Atkinson 1978).

Newcomers to sociology may find it difficult to make much sense of ethnomethodology. Many old hands find it an extraordinarily obscure, though fascinating, activity. For the purposes of this book, the important point to grasp is that it is a way of studying social life that concentrates on the unwritten rules that make ordinary everyday social activity orderly, and tries to spell out these rules. The main methods of data collection are observation and recording including the use of both sound and videotape.

Activity

Gomm and McNeill (1982), Items 55 and 56, includes several suggestions for a simple kind of ethnomethodological research. Some overlap into ordinary ethnography, and therefore appear on p. 73 of this book. The particularly ethnomethodological suggestions include some Garfinkel-type experiments for disrupting social order, but with a warning that there are ethical problems involved in experiments such as disrupting family life by acting as a lodger in your own home.

6

Secondary data

The data that is used by sociologists may be 'primary' or 'secondary'. Primary data is collected by the researcher at first hand, mainly through surveys, interviews, or participant observation. 'Secondary' data is available from some other source, and comes in various forms.

Data from earlier sociological research

Sometimes, a researcher can use data from previous studies as the basis for new work. Blauner (1964), in his study of the experiences of different types of factory worker, brought together empirical evidence from several sources. He used data from job-attitude surveys carried out in 1947 and 1959, from a study of an automobile factory published in 1959, and from several case-studies. He also carried out a small enquiry of his own.

Halsey and his colleagues (1980) wished to 'reconstruct the education experienced by children passing through schools and colleges in England and Wales as they have developed since before the First World War'. To do this, they adapted material from a survey conducted into social mobility (Goldthorpe 1980), using it to focus on their particular concerns.

Statistics

Official statistics

The phrase 'official statistics' refers to statistics collected by the state and its agencies. They are assembled in various ways.

The Census In the United Kingdom, this is held every ten years (i.e. 1961, 1971, 1981), and involves distributing a questionnaire to every household. It is therefore a full survey conducted on the whole population. The head of each household, which includes people who are in charge of residential homes, hotels, etc., is required by law to fill in the questionnaire on behalf of everybody in the household, or at least to ensure that they fill in one for themselves. The questionnaire varies from one Census to another, but always includes questions about age, sex, and the relationships of the members of the household. It also asks about their work, their educational qualifications, and whether they have moved house in recent years. The Census includes questions about living accommodation. How many rooms are there? What sanitary facilities are there? Recent Censuses have included questions about the birthplace of members of the household, but attempts to introduce an 'ethnic question', to find out the size of the ethnic minorities resident in this country, have so far been unsuccessful. Contrary to a common misunderstanding, the Census asks nothing about wealth or income.

Activity

If you live in England or Wales, and would like to study the Census results for your locality, obtain the Small Area

Statistics for your home town from: Census Customer Services, OPCS, Titchfield, Fareham, Hants PO15 5RR. Tel.: 0329 42511 ext. 231 and 296.

Registration In the United Kingdom, certain life events have to be registered by law. The most obvious examples are births, marriages, and deaths. These figures are collected continuously, and at any particular moment details of what is happening can be worked out. This contrasts with the Census, which is a snapshot of the situation every ten years.

State surveys other than the Census The state conducts several other surveys at regular intervals, all of them on a sample basis. The General Household Survey is conducted annually, and the Family Expenditure Survey and New Earnings Survey are commissioned by government departments and carried out by the Office of Population Censuses and Surveys.

Central Statistical Office Many aspects of the state's activities involve the routine collection of statistics, and these are regularly published in booklets. There are literally hundreds of these, and you should look at a catalogue of the Central Statistical Office to see what is available. Some familiar examples include crime statistics, unemployment statistics, education statistics, and economic statistics.

Activity

During one month, make a note of the occasions when a news item (TV, radio, or newspaper) is based on the publication of an official statistical report. Try to find out how the statistics quoted were collected, and how to obtain a copy of the report.

These statistics are most readily available in two annual compendiums: the *Annual Abstract of Statistics* and *Social*

94

Trends. Both are expensive, but both will be available in all public libraries, and in most larger school and college libraries. The former is a collection of the more interesting statistics published by the state, and the latter is made up from the same sources, but is presented in a more varied and readable form, including charts and diagrams. It includes short articles summing up some of the main changes that have taken place and which are apparent in the tables.

In any large, complex, and centralized state, these figures are needed for planning and evaluating social policy. For example, knowing how many people aged between fifty and sixty are alive today, together with knowledge about the death-rate of this age group and their state of health, enables the state to plan the number of places that may be needed in residential homes for the elderly in twenty years' time, as well as the level of home help provision that will be necessary. This does not automatically mean that the provision will be made, but it does make it possible to plan in the light of solid knowledge rather than guesswork. Any state that has a system of publicly funded welfare – and all modern industrial societies do – needs information about the population it is dealing with.

Activity

Borrow a copy of the *Annual Abstract* or *Social Trends*. Note the range of statistics that are included. Look at the footnotes to the tables to see all the different ways in which the statistics were collected. Think of ways in which the various statistics might be used by policy-makers.

Other sources of statistics

Agencies other than the state produce statistics that may be useful for sociological research. Most large pressure groups run or commission surveys on their own special interests. Trade unions will usually have statistical data about the industries in which their members are working. Any commercial organization that is quoted on the Stock Exchange is supposed to publish a statement of its financial affairs annually, and these can provide a wealth of information for sociologists who are interested in economic affairs.

How can sociologists use official statistics?

Many sociologists take these statistics at their face value, and use them as a ready-made source of data for their research. They are cheap, readily available, cover a long time-span, and are comprehensive in their coverage of social life. They may be the only source of data on the topic in question, and they make it possible to do 'before-and-after' studies. For example, a study could be made of the impact of some piece of legislation, such as the Abortion Act or the Divorce Law Reform Act of 1971.

However, there may be problems. Since the statistics are collected for administrative rather than sociological purposes, the definitions used and the classifications made are often unsuitable. It is not easy to make all the correlations that are needed. It is not possible to check the accuracy of the figures. While it is probable that the number of births recorded is as accurate as we are likely to need, the records of some social events are, by their nature, likely to be incomplete.

The best example of this is crime statistics. Clearly, many crimes go unrecorded, either because they are undiscovered, or because they are not reported to the police. Many crimes depend for their success on being undiscovered, such as fraud and embezzlement. Others are not reported because of embarrassment or fear on the part of the victim (rape, domestic assaults), or because he or she thinks that there is little the police can do about it (vandalism, shoplifting), or that the offence is not very serious anyway, or that there is no unwilling victim (drug abuse, soliciting, under-age sex). Even when crimes are discovered and reported, they are not always recorded. It seems that the police record about two-thirds of the property crime that comes to their attention, and about half of the violent crime.

Various techniques have been developed to respond to the problem of incomplete crime statistics, of which 'victim surveys' and 'self-report' studies are the most common. In a 'victim survey', such as the British Crime Survey of 1983, a sample of the population is asked to give details of any crime of which they have been a victim in the previous year. 'Self-report' studies are anonymous questionnaire-based surveys which invite people to say what crimes they have themselves committed. Both types of survey show a far higher figure for crimes committed than do the official statistics produced by the police. They reveal the 'dark number' of crimes, which varies widely from one type of crime to another. The British Crime Survey found that only about 8 per cent of incidents of vandalism were recorded in the official statistics, compared with 48 per cent of burglaries, and 100 per cent of thefts of motor-vehicles.

Further variation in the crime figures will be caused by alterations in the law, and by changes in police practice, perhaps in response to public opinion, which is itself fed by the published statistics.

A great deal of work has been done in attempts to get at the 'true' total of crimes committed. Such work, however, rests on the assumption that there is such a figure, waiting to be accurately counted if only the right techniques can be developed. In the case of, say, births and deaths, this is certainly the case, but most social statistics are not like this. Instead, they are the result of people making a series of decisions about what has happened. Most health statistics, for example, are the result of people deciding that they are ill, and successfully convincing a doctor of this. If the doctor does not agree with them, then they do not go into the health statistics produced by the National Health Service. In other cases the doctor may, as a result of a routine check, say you are ill even though you do not feel it. Again, it is the doctor's decision that produces the statistic.

Some sociologists have made a special study of these 'statistic-producing' processes. They treat the statistics as a topic for sociological analysis rather than a resource for theory-building. Again, crime statistics are a good example of the process. The sequence of decisions that produces a crime statistic may be presented diagrammatically, as in *Figure 5*.

Figure 5 The social construction of criminal statistics

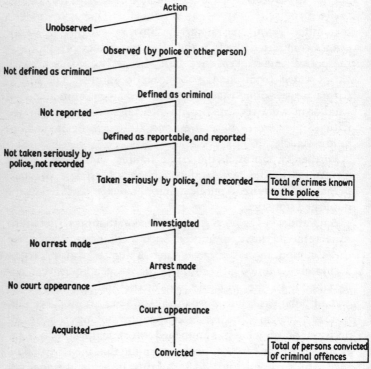

Source: McNeill and Townley (1981)

'At every stage, the police and other social actors are making decisions about what action to take, based on their definition of the situation. Decisions are made by reference to a combination of common-sense assumptions, experience, and professional expertise concerning crime and criminals, public opinion, expectations of fellow-officers and superiors, the chance of securing a conviction, and other factors.'   (McNeill and Townley 1981)

A critical view

So far, we have seen the argument that is put forward by those who stress that official statistics are constructed rather than merely collected.

Sociologists influenced by a more Marxist approach accept the importance of this work, but maintain that it does not go far enough. For them, the important point is that these figures are produced by the state. The state is seen not as a neutral body, but as the key agency in the promotion of the interests and values of the ruling class in capitalist society. They wish to show how official statistics (state-istics) contribute to keeping the dominant class in power, by presenting information in ways which do not harm their interests.

They are not saying that the Central Statistical Office is engaged in some deep-laid plot against the working class. Rather they argue that, since the role of the state is to defend and justify the capitalist system, then official statistics must play their part in this.

At one level, this may simply be a matter of 'massaging' the statistics, something in which all governments engage. You do not have to be a Marxist to see that the official statistics of unemployment include only those who are signing on at Job Centres and are eligible for benefit. They therefore exclude married women, people who have retired early, those on Youth Training Schemes and other Manpower Services Commission courses, those who have returned unwillingly to school because they cannot find jobs, those on short-time work, and others. When the 1971 Census asked a question about employment status, it found that about 40 per cent more people regarded themselves as unemployed than the official statistics showed.

99

A more subtle aspect of this argument concerns which statistics are collected and which are not. There is a great deal of information available about fire damage to property, but little on diseases related to industrial work. The figures on homelessness are vague and misleading, but those on new homes constructed are carefully recorded. We know more about social security 'scrounging' than we do about income tax evasion. We know more about the poor, who have to fill in forms of all kinds in order to receive benefits, than we do about the rich, who have to declare their tax position only to the taxman, in strict confidence.

Then there is the way in which the statistics are presented. The Registrar-General's scale of social class, used throughout the Census reports, is based on the employment of the head of the household. From a Marxist standpoint this ignores and therefore obscures the real basis of social class, which is the ownership of productive wealth.

Another line of argument emphasizes how women are rendered invisible in these statistics. In addition to being under-counted in the unemployment figures, a woman's class is determined by that of her husband, all tables are presented with the male figures first, the 'head of the household' definition systematically favours men, and housework is not classified as work.

Using examples such as these, it is argued that the processes by which statistics are produced, or not produced, and the way they are presented, follow a pattern that is organized around the exploitation of one class and sex by another in capitalist society.

Activities

1 Draw diagrams like the one in *Figure 5* to show how statistics are produced on the following: suicide; strikes; battered wives; divorce.

2 Look again at the explanation of the concepts of reliability and validity (pp. 12–13). Consider the reliability and the

validity of different kinds of official statistics in the light of the above discussion.

Documents as secondary data

Besides the statistics discussed above, there is a rich source of data available to sociologists among the many personal and public documents that exist in a literate and record-keeping society.

Personal documents

These include letters, diaries, and autobiographies. These are first-person descriptions of social events, written by an individual who was involved in or witnessed those happenings. They include the writer's attitudes towards the events. As sources of evidence, the sociologist shares them with the historian. Roberts (1971) is a rather special example, in that it combines personal reminiscence with careful historical research into poverty in Edwardian Manchester.

The first major piece of sociological work that relied on personal documents was Thomas and Znaniecki's *The Polish Peasant in Europe and America* (1919). In this study of the migration of Polish peasants to the USA, Thomas and Znaniecki relied heavily on first-hand accounts supplied by people who had been directly involved. These included letters and diaries, as well as life-histories obtained in interview (see p. 85).

Sociologists who use such documents have to ask themselves whether the evidence therein is authentic, whether it is complete, how representative it is of the experiences described, whether it is distorted by the personal bias of the writer, and why it was written. Material written in the expectation that it will be published is going to be different from material that is never expected to be read by anyone other than the author and perhaps a close friend. For this reason, the diaries of prominent politicians, such as those of Richard Crossman or Harold

Wilson, have to be read with some scepticism, as they tend to be self-justificatory. Similarly, autobiographies may be idealized, though private letters and diaries are likely to be genuine enough.

Public documents

In modern societies written records are kept by all kinds of agencies, and some may be available to social researchers. In order to protect the privacy of those whose lives are recorded, the material may be kept confidential for some years, or may be available only in a form where individuals cannot be identified. Such documents include school records, parish records, social work records, health records, police records, court records, and other records kept by government agencies. There are also the minutes of meetings, whether of local clubs and societies or of councils and parliament itself. Commercial firms, too, keep records of their decision-making procedures and financial transactions. Not all these are easily or indeed ever available to outsiders, but they should still be considered as potential sources of data.

Further reading

Gomm and McNeill (1982), Item 47, shows how it is possible to use secondary sources to find out about local companies and the local labour market.

There are also official histories that are commissioned by government, as well as the official reports of public enquiries. It is interesting to speculate on how future social researchers will use the Scarman Report into the civil unrest in British cities in 1981, or the various enquiries that have been held into aspects of the events in Northern Ireland. The Black Report into inequalities in health (Townsend and Davidson 1982) has already passed into the main body of research, though it was commissioned and published, albeit unwillingly, by government.

Local authorities in England and Wales have all had to produce 'structure plans' about planned development in their area. These provide a mass of well-presented data about the area, and can be used in all kinds of local studies. Ideas can be found in Gomm and McNeill (1982), Item 46.

Other possible sources of research data are the official handbooks and prospectuses published by any large organization that is anxious to inform the general public, selectively, about its activities. Those of you who are involved in deciding whether to apply for a place in further or higher education will already know a good deal about how to read prospectuses without believing everything they say: what they do not say is just as important. What is sociologically interesting about them is the assumptions that underlie what they say about themselves, and what image they are trying to project.

The mass media provide a further source of material for research. TV and radio programmes, especially news broadcasts, have been extensively studied, as have newspaper reports. Letters to the editor, including agony columns, tell us something about the concerns people have, or at least which of their concerns are considered by editors and agony aunties to be suitable for publication.

Novels can be of interest to sociology. Charles Dickens provides us with a vivid account of nineteenth-century urban poverty in such novels as *Oliver Twist* and *Great Expectations*. Semi-autobiographical novels, like Richard Llewellyn's *How Green Was My Valley*, an account of life in South Wales mining villages, and Richard Gordon's humorous *Doctor* stories about the medical profession, can give unique insights. Anyone who reads E. M. Forster's *A Passage to India* will gain a better understanding of the impact of imperial power on personal relationships. Novels can also be used as a topic for study in themselves, quite apart from their value as data to be used in studies of the social worlds which they describe.

Such sources are valuable for the wide-ranging data they provide and, particularly, for the historical dimension they add to primary data that is necessarily bound to the present day. Care has to be taken when using them, however. The sociologist has to consider the following questions:

Is the material authentic? Is it any way a forgery?

Is the material factually accurate? Are any errors deliberate or accidental?

Is the material reliable? Would it have been the same if it had been collected by anyone else? What personal biases and distortions are likely to be present?

Is it systematic, providing a complete account of what it describes? What is it lacking?

Why was it collected? Was it a matter of routine, or was there some specific, possibly propagandist purpose?

Is the material representative? Written records of the past, for example, will by definition have been written by the literate, and they were an unrepresentative minority of the population. Only the reasonably wealthy kept diaries or wrote letters to each other.

Of course, there is no way that the reader can answer any of these questions with certainty, but they should be borne in mind. It is interesting to note, in passing, that most of them are questions that have to be asked of primary data as well.

Content analysis

All this mass of secondary material can be utilized in many ways. It may be used just to give the researcher a feel for what is being studied; as a resource to back up or complement evidence produced from other sources; or as evidence in itself, as the topic of the research.

In this last case, at least, the material will need to be considered systematically, and the most usual way of doing this is through content analysis. This is a method of analysing the contents of documents or other non-statistical material in such a way that it is possible to make statistical comparisons between them.

For example, many feminist sociologists have made content analyses of children's books, to highlight how boys are usually shown in active, creative, practical roles, whereas girls are shown as passive, domestic, and as followers rather than leaders. This involves creating a list of categories such as 'takes lead' or 'follows', 'gives orders' or 'obeys orders', 'works out of doors' or 'works indoors', 'mends car' or 'does housework', and counting up each occasion on which the characters in the book do these things. In some traditional reading books there was a clear assumption that boys were leaders and girls were followers. More recently, books have been written which try to avoid these stereotypes.

Newspapers and television have been a popular subject for content analysis. The Glasgow University Media Group's research into television news relied heavily on the technique. They videotaped all TV news bulletins in the early months of 1975, and then spent a year analysing the stories into categories such as parliamentary politics, Northern Ireland, terrorism, demonstrations, Labour Party internal, crime, economics (currency), economics (business), sport, and many more. In fact, they had great difficulty in producing a satisfactory list of categories, and had to revise it as work progressed. Their research produced statistical evidence of the way in which TV news systematically favoured certain points of view of current events, rather than maintaining the balance that was claimed (Glasgow University Media Group 1976).

Activities

1 Carry out a content analysis of every newspaper published on a certain day. (Share the expense among a group of students.) Use your figures to show how the pattern of reporting varies systematically from one paper to another.

2 Carry out a content analysis of one evening's TV viewing, showing how women are portrayed. You may want to

105

concentrate on entertainment programmes, on advertisements, or on news and current affairs. You will have to devise a list of categories such as 'housewife', 'sex symbol', 'career woman', 'nag', etc. Some characters will fall into more than one category.

7

Theory, science, and values

This chapter will pick up points raised earlier in the book and take them further. It is not concerned so much with how research is done, but rather with some of the more abstract arguments surrounding sociological research.

Theoretical issues

Anybody who wishes to study any aspect of the world about them has to decide what methods they are going to use. Their decision is made on the basis of their assumptions about what kind of thing it is that they are studying. Scientists who study the natural world, including plants, minerals, and animals, assume that the things they are studying are not aware of their own existence, and that the causes of their behaviour are outside their control. They do not choose to behave as they do. Accordingly, they can be studied on the assumption that everything there is to be known about them can be found through observation of their external behaviour.

In social science, the question of the consciousness and awareness of what is being studied lies at the root of the debate between 'positivism' and 'phenomenology'.

Positivism

Positivism is a philosophical concept, and refers to a particular set of assumptions about the world and about appropriate ways of studying it. These assumptions were set out on p. 41, in the discussion of experiments, and you should look at them again now. They are the basis of the natural science that we are used to in western cultures.

This approach to the study of the natural world was at its most influential during the eighteenth and nineteenth centuries, and was certainly vindicated by the scientific discoveries made during that period, and by the successes of Victorian civil and mechanical engineers, and in the fields of public health and medicine. It seemed clear that there was a body of knowledge that existed independently of whether people knew it or not, and that the task of the scientist was to uncover that knowledge piece by piece, building up a more complete understanding of the laws of nature.

Given the success of natural science during the nineteenth century, it is hardly surprising that such theorists as Marx and Durkheim followed this approach in their studies of the social world. Positivist sociology, like positivist natural science, assumes that there are laws that govern the operations of the social world, and that use of the appropriate methods of analysis will uncover these laws. They can then be described in an objective and value-free way. Social behaviour and events are seen as the result of external pressures acting on people, who are relatively passive in their response to such pressures. Predictions about the social world can be made, and this makes possible a certain amount of social engineering. This should lead to a reduction of poverty, or crime, or social unrest, or whatever it is that the writer believes is an undesirable aspect of human affairs. In other words, there is absolute truth and it can be used to create a better society. The truth is value-free and objective, but it is sought with the intention of using it in ways that accord with the values of the scientist. In Marx's case, this meant the revolutionary overthrow of the established capitalist order. For Durkheim, greater social stability was desirable, achieved through the promotion of what he called 'organic solidarity'.

The positivist approach to the study of the social world continued to be influential in sociology up to the 1960s. It was by no means the only approach, but it was the one that had the most status, and sociologists were anxious to establish their new discipline in the academic world.

It was this tradition that led to the development of sociological research methods that concentrate on producing supposedly 'objective' data, usually in the form of statistics. In natural science, as we have seen on p. 42, the conventional form of an experiment is based on the hypothetico-deductive method. (If necessary, look at this again now.) The experiment is the best way of following this procedure but, failing that, collecting data in the real world is the next best thing. From a positivist standpoint, the more objective such data the better. The important thing is to develop methods of data collection that are as objective as those in natural science. If the data produced is quantitative, i.e. in the form of numbers and statistics, then various tests can be carried out on it and causal correlations established.

Many surveys that set out to explain some social phenomenon have been modelled on these lines. The survey is designed to test an hypothesis, just as in an experiment. Statistical data is collected, and tests performed on it to test the original hypothesis.

A clear example of this is Blauner (1964). He wished to investigate industrial workers' experience of alienation in the workplace. He hypothesized that different levels of alienation are causally linked with different types of industrial process.

Having operationalized the concept of alienation, he then measured its presence in four different industrial contexts. For Blauner, technology and the social environment of the workplace are the independent variables (causes), and alienation is the dependent variable (effect) (see p. 92). His evidence showed, to his satisfaction, that the hypothesized link was present. He was therefore able to forecast that levels of alienation would decrease as technological processes became more automated since, as he saw it, those working with this new technology would regain a sense of dignity and personal worth.

An extreme example of this approach is that of the Gluecks, who set out to identify the causes of juvenile crime by making detailed studies of 500 delinquents in American reform schools, and comparing the results with those from 500 youngsters who, because they were not in reform schools, were assumed to be law-abiding. The Gluecks conclude that a combination of factors (physical, temperamental, attitudinal, intellectual, and socio-cultural) causes delinquency, and that 'future delinquency can be successfully foretold in some nine-tenths of the cases' (Glueck and Glueck 1964).

In this kind of research, the main priorities for the researcher are that there should be no suspicion that the data collected has been affected by the values of the researcher, and that it is completely reliable. In other words, it should be possible to claim that whoever collected the data would have arrived at similar conclusions. Whether at the level of small groups or of whole societies, the sociologist is aiming to identify the laws that govern human social behaviour, and so to explain it.

Phenomenology and interpretive sociology

As already stated, Marx, Durkheim, and other classical sociologists were much influenced by positivist approaches to scientific study. But another of the classical sociologists, Max Weber, had reservations about this approach.

Weber argued that there is an important difference between the subject matter of sociology and the subject matter of the natural sciences. This important difference is that man is an active, conscious being, aware of what is going on in a social situation, and capable of making choices about how to act. Natural phenomena have no meaning for those involved in them. What makes a social event social is that all those involved give it the same meaning. They all interpret what is happening in broadly the same way. If they do not, social interaction cannot take place. If we are to explain some event in the social world, our explanation has to take into account what the people involved feel and think about it. We must not regard them simply as helpless puppets.

Durkheim, of course, knew perfectly well that people have insight and understanding of what is going on around them, but his explanations of social phenomena did not stress this aspect of social life. Weber believed that it was not enough just to show the external causes. It was also necessary to show how these causes actually influenced people's thinking about the world. Thus, in his explanation of the growth of capitalism (see p. 51), he showed not only that Calvinism was the independent variable that was only present in Europe, and thus was an important cause of the rise of capitalism, but he also went to great pains to spell out why it was that a belief in Calvinism would make someone behave in the way he described. The explanation is adequate at the level of meaning, just as much as at the level of cause.

This emphasis on meaning and consciousness is also a central feature of the sociology of the Chicago School, influenced as it was by the theories of George Mead, a philosopher at that university. Mead was especially interested in the concept of self, and delivered a series of lectures in the 1920s which were later published as *Mind, Self and Society*. In these lectures, Mead argued that a sense of self, of who one is in relation to others, can only develop in a social context. Children have to learn to 'take the attitude of the other', that is, they have to learn to see the social world as others see it. We all have to learn to put ourselves in other people's shoes (or, to put it more vividly, to get inside other people's heads), if we are to interact socially. The central feature of social life is that actions are the result of people's interpretations of the situation that they are in. People interpret the actions of others, and react according to that interpretation. Most of the time, such interpretations are shared by all those involved and social life proceeds smoothly enough. There are, however, occasions when interpretations differ, and more or less serious social breakdown occurs. The causes of social action lie in people's 'definition of the situation', their interpretation of events, not in some pattern of objective laws that govern from outside.

It follows that, if we want to explain social actions, we have first to understand them in the way that the participants do. We must learn to see the world from their standpoint. We must develop research methods that make it possible for us to do this. This is the tradition of social research that has given rise to ethnographic studies, particularly the technique of participant observation. Data collected in this way is qualitative in form rather than quantitative, that is, it concentrates on presenting the quality of the way of life described rather than on presenting statistics. Qualitative data is in the form of words rather than numbers. Much of the research report is composed of word-for-word quotation from those being studied.

These interpretive methods became even more popular with the emergence and growth of phenomenological sociology in the 1960s. Phenomenology, like positivism, is a philosophy in its own right which has been applied to the study of sociology. Edmund Husserl (1859–1938) founded phenomenology in the early part of the twentieth century, and Alfred Schutz (1899–1959) applied Husserl's ideas to the study of social life. Schutz's work, in turn, was brought to a wider audience by Berger and Luckmann in their book *The Social Construction of Reality* (1967). They argue that social reality is not out there, waiting to be experienced by social actors, even though it may often feel as though it is. Instead, we actively create (or construct) social reality through social interaction. It then takes on the appearance of existing independently of us, and is perceived as influencing our behaviour from outside. Berger and Luckmann discuss how social actors construct reality, and the way in which they then experience this reality as external to them. While much of their discussion is highly theoretical, it has given rise to research into how reality is constructed at an everyday level. This approach has led some sociologists into ethnomethodology, which has been described on pp. 88–91.

All these influences, taken together and separately, have led to the growth of those research methods that emphasize the importance of studying social life in its natural setting, and describing it as it is seen and experienced by those involved. The emphasis of these methods is on the validity of the data collected, which may be achieved at the price of its reliability or its representativeness. Social reality is seen as 'intersubjective', i.e. it exists in the shared consciousness of actors. It is not objective or external, but is a construction of shared meanings and interpretations. Man is a conscious, active, purposeful social being, rather than being subject to external influences over which he has no control. The task of sociological research is to describe these shared meanings, which may, in turn, make it possible to explain why people behave as they do.

The range of methods

As we have already seen, most research studies employ more than one method of data collection, but they usually have a clear preference for one or the other of the two major research styles, survey research or ethnography, producing quantitative or qualitative data. However, it is important not to think of the two styles as falling into two completely separate compartments. It is better to think of them as being on a scale, as shown in *Figure 6*.

On this scale, it is apparent that the more people who are studied, the less the researcher becomes personally involved with them. If the researcher thinks personal involvement is important, the price to be paid is that fewer people can be studied. Where the survey researcher may claim reliability and

Figure 6   Methods of data collection

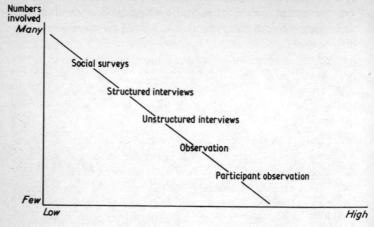

Source: Worsley (1977:89)

representativeness, the ethnographer will claim validity. The survey enthusiast will point out the dangers of bias and unreliability in ethnography, and stress how the representativeness of a sample can be calculated precisely. The ethnographer may concede all this, but would point out that it is not much use being able to produce the same results over and over again, and to say how representative they are, if they are invalid in the first place. The questionnaire may produce the same statistics whenever it is used, but this may be just a matter of repeating the same distortions. The survey style of research imposes a structure on that which is being researched, rather than allowing the structure to emerge from the data as it is collected. A survey can collect data only about those things which are included in the questionnaire, and this may omit crucial points. An ethnographic study, on the other hand, can never be repeated in exactly the same way, so there is no way of checking its findings.

With the apparent ending of British sociology's 'wars of

religion' (see p. 6), most researchers would now accept that it is sensible to use a mixture of methods, and to use the strengths of one method to compensate for the weaknesses of another. This approach is summed up most clearly by Howard Newby:

'The methodology was deliberately eclectic, involving the routine perusal of agricultural and population census statistics, a search of historical sources (both documentary and oral), participant observation and a survey investigation. Since many of the concerns of the study involve the interrelationships of farmers and farmworkers and of farmworkers with each other, it was apparent from the outset that a degree of participant observation would be necessary. However, the almost complete lack of any sociologically relevant data, even of a sociographic kind, made it desirable to conduct a survey. In effect, the survey and the period of participant observation increasingly came to complement each other: insights gained from participant observation could be checked against survey data; on the other hand much of this data could often only become meaningful through the experiences gained from living with a farmworker and his family in a tied cottage for six months and gaining first-hand knowledge about the work and community situation.' (Newby 1977)

Some contemporary writers refer to this process as 'triangulation'. This is a term borrowed from land surveying, and means simply that you get a better view of things by looking at them from more than one direction. Though some writers suggest that this is a new approach, it has been widespread in sociology for years. Virtually all the studies listed on p. 40 and on p. 72 use multiple methods.

In terms of theory, all this ties in with the recognition that, while people's actions are a result of their interpretation of a situation, their interpretations and their choices are limited by structural factors external to them and beyond their control.

For an exercise designed to show how positivist and interpretive approaches affect the conclusions drawn from statistical data, see Gomm and McNeill (1982), Item 7.

Practical issues

While the theoretical debates outlined above have great influence on the choice of research method, practical issues must not be forgotten. These are not wholly distinct from theory, but can be stated rather more briefly. The main ones are time, labour, power, money, and choice of topic.

All social research takes time, but a study based on participant observation usually requires at least two years. In most such studies, the researcher or team of researchers spends between six months and two years 'in the field', and there is then a long period of analysing the data and writing the research report. There is no short cut possible in any of this. Writing up transcripts of interviews and identifying themes is just a lengthy business. Of course, in most such studies the researcher has begun to identify themes, classify, and index the data while the research is still in progress, but there is always a great deal more to be done. And even then there will be another year to wait before a book is published.

Survey-based research is usually quicker to carry out. It is important not to rush it, but once the questionnaire or interview schedule has been finalized, data collection can proceed quite quickly and, if the questionnaire has been well designed, data analysis presents less of a problem since statistics can be processed with the help of a computer. The writing of the report still has to be done but, taken all in all, surveys can usually be completed in a shorter time than can ethnographic research. There are exceptions. Townsend's study *Poverty in the United Kingdom*, published in 1979, was based on research carried out in 1969.

The size of the research team will have an important bearing on the research method chosen. In survey research, a lone researcher would simply not have the time to carry out large numbers of face-to-face interviews and process the resulting data. In ethnography, a lone researcher can only become involved with a relatively small group of people, or a clearly delimited social context such as a classroom. If labour power is in short supply the research is likely to take the form of a small survey, or a case-study, or perhaps be based on secondary data.

Time and labour power usually boil down to a matter of money. If there is enough money to pay salaries, either more time can be taken or a larger research team created, which can do the same amount of work more quickly. Clearly, the larger the team that can be trained to administer an interview schedule, the larger the sample that can be questioned. In the case of ethnography, the financial question is largely a matter of how long the researcher's salary and living expenses can be met. If there is plenty of money, then a team of ethnographers can work together, as in Becker's studies (Becker *et al.* 1961, 1968), or in the Banbury restudy (Stacey 1975). The question of the funding of research was discussed on p. 10.

There is a four-cornered relationship between theoretical preferences, choice of topic (also discussed on p. 10), practical considerations, and choice of research method, as shown in *Figure 7*.

A sociologist's theoretical perspective will guide the choice of topic and research method adopted. Choice of topic influences research method and vice versa. Time, money, and

Figure 7 Choice of research topic

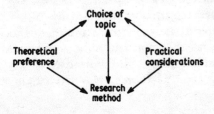

labour power will in turn determine what is realistically possible.

Activity

Which research methods could be used in the study of the following topics:

Divorce	Queueing	Courtship patterns
Exam failure	Poverty	Single parenting
Rock concerts	Racism	Ageing

How would the research method be affected if the researcher was (a) a lone student on a research grant? (b) the leader of a team of four researchers with funding guaranteed for three years?

Sociology, science, and values

Is sociology a science?

Until fairly recently, this question was of great importance to sociologists. As we have seen (pp. 108–13), the success of nineteenth-century science prompted the classical sociologists to stress that a science of society was both possible and desirable, and that such a science should be closely modelled on the natural sciences. It was not until the 1960s that this urge to be 'scientific' was widely questioned, and two factors prompted this questioning.

The first was the revival, described above, of interpretative and phenomenological perspectives in sociology, which stressed the difference, first emphasized by Weber, between the subject matter of natural science and that of social science. If you believe that the important thing about social action is the meaning that it has for those involved in it, then you will want to approach it in a different way from that of the natural sciences.

The second factor was the changing view of what was actually involved in studying natural science. After the certainties and the optimism of the nineteenth century, science has had a much rougher ride during this century. We are now more aware of the possible abuse of scientific knowledge, and of the sometimes disastrous side-effects of the things that are done to the environment in the name of scientific progress. We know that scientists have sometimes been wrong, and this knowledge has led to some loss of status for natural science.

Philosophers of science have also questioned the accounts of how natural science research is done. The hypothetico-deductive model (see p. 42) portrays scientific research as a coldly logical process, proceeding step by step in a rational manner. It appears to generate more and more knowledge, gradually increasing the total of human understanding of the natural world, which is there, waiting to be understood and explained.

This account sounds convincing but has been challenged by many writers, including numbers of practising scientists. They point out that many discoveries are made almost by accident, and that insight, imagination, and luck all play a crucial role in scientific research. The logical account can only be written after the research has been completed. It certainly does not feel like that at the time.

Kuhn (1970) has taken the debate in another direction. He argues that scientists normally work within a set of assumptions about what the natural world is like. These are not questioned, but are taken for granted as correct. He calls this a 'paradigm' and says that normal science operates within paradigms which guide the selection and evaluation of evidence. As time passes, more and more evidence appears that does not fit the paradigm. At first it is ignored or explained away, but eventually becomes so numerous that the paradigm is overthrown in a 'scientific revolution'. A new paradigm is established, and normal science resumes.

Kuhn's point is that natural scientific knowledge does not exist independently and objectively, but is constructed and created by scientists within a framework of assumptions. The

119

central theme of the sociology of knowledge is that all knowledge is a product of its social context, and will therefore vary from one context to another. It is produced rather than discovered. This is easy to accept when we are talking about history or literature, but some would argue that natural science is essentially no different from these other forms of knowledge.

The familiar word 'data' illustrates the point. 'Data' means, literally, 'things that are given', i.e. there, waiting to be found. It assumes a positivist view of the world. But if knowledge is created and constructed, then data is not 'given', but produced. We need a different word, which stresses how knowledge is a product, not a given. Every research method is a means of *producing* knowledge, not *collecting* it. None simply records 'the facts' or 'the truth' as an external object.

Whether or not sociology is a science depends on what is meant by science. The best answer to this is to see science as a method rather than a body of knowledge. What distinguishes both social and natural science from non-science, from common sense and from ideology, is method. Good sociology is logically derived from empirical evidence. The evidence, and how it was collected, are made available to others who can check the conclusions that have been drawn. Sociologists are not the only people capable of producing insights into how the social world operates, but they have been trained in a rigorous and critical way of thinking, which demands that nothing is ever taken on trust but is always subjected to critical examination in the light of all the evidence available. Sociologists are usually their own strongest critics, and these internal disputes are sometimes seen as a sign of the weakness of the discipline. They are not weaknesses, but strengths, in a discipline that is rooted in critical analysis.

The desire to show that sociology was as scientific as natural science claimed to be has resulted in the accounts of how research was done being very idealized. Writers were often so concerned to match up to an impossible ideal that their accounts are of what they thought should have happened and people expected to read, rather than frank descriptions of what

120

actually happened. While this book has stressed the importance of reading these works in the original, it is also important to read them critically, trying to visualize the reality behind the written version.

This situation has changed recently. As both natural and social scientists have become more prepared to acknowledge what research is really like, so several collections of papers have appeared that give a 'warts and all' account of research studies previously published. Examples of this are Bell and Newby (1977), Hammond (1964), and Shipman (1976). The publication of Malinowski's (1967) personal diaries has also shown how great was the gap between his public accounts and his private feelings. In addition, recent original studies often now include a frank account of the trials and tribulations of the research, including a statement about the researcher's own background, since this is acknowledged to have an important bearing on the validity and the reliability of the research. Such accounts do not necessarily cast doubt on the scientific status of the work done. If the ideal of natural scientific method is in fact a myth, then sociologists cannot be criticized for failing to match up to it. Instead, we have to revise our view of what science is.

Values

This last point takes us into a discussion of values. The nineteenth-century positivist sociologists, as we have seen, believed that their task was to discover the laws of social development in order that a better society could be created. They had no reservations about the idea that the purpose of discovering the truth was to improve things, in whatever field.

In the twentieth century, developments in positivism led to the belief that facts could and should be separated from values. The scientist's task is to identify scientific laws, and that is all. The notion of a search for objective and value-free knowledge became identified with a belief that the scientist should be morally indifferent as to how the knowledge was used. This

121

view has come under attack in its turn. This debate is very complex, and can only be simplified here.

Those who believe that there is no objectively existing truth, independent of its context, will argue that any claim to value-free knowledge is a nonsense. A more widely held view is that there can be value-free truth, but that this still leaves the question: 'At what points in the research process is it permissible for values to play a part, and at what points should they be controlled or eliminated?'

As we have seen in the quotation from Halsey, Heath, and Ridge (1980) on p. 11, most sociologists accept the position first spelled out by Weber: that choice of topic must be influenced by values, both personal and related to historical context, but that such value-commitment should not stretch to the methods used. Science requires that all the evidence should be considered, not just a selection from it, and logical analysis must take precedence over moral convictions. If the results are not what the researcher would have liked them to be, that is just too bad. However, while the researcher must avoid bias in his work, this does mean that moral indifference can be accepted.

This takes us back to the question, 'What is sociology for?' (see p. 8). Some sociologists maintain that the task of sociology is just to increase our understanding of social life:

'It may be the case that if we can increase our understanding of a social problem, then we put ourselves in a better position to do something about it. But in doing something about it, we are no longer operating as sociologists, as students of social life: we are operating as social reformers, as politicians, or as citizens. As sociologists, all we can do is to study social life as carefully and as competently as we can.'   (Cuff and Payne 1984)

Others would argue that, since it is inevitable that values affect the work we do, the important thing is to be clear about what those values are. Becker (1967) posed this question as, 'Whose side are we on?' All knowledge must favour somebody, he argues, and therefore we have to choose who to favour. His answer is that sociologists should favour the 'under-dogs', the people whose voices are seldom or never heard in public debate, because they are powerless to make themselves heard. Participant observation research of deviant groups enables their point of view to be expressed.

Gouldner (1973) wrote of the 'myth of a value-free sociology'. He maintains that this myth has enabled sociologists to evade the moral implications of the work they do, and to avoid offending the powers-that-be. Moral indifference is, he affirms, a deeply immoral stance to take up.

This leads to a more radical view, which says that it is not enough merely to help people have their say. This does not change their situation. What is needed is a sociology that will show people who are oppressed how to throw off their oppressors. It should be a committed sociology, whose intention is radical or revolutionary change in society, and a fundamental change in power structures. This does not mean that the work is any less scientific, but it is committed to a particular value position.

Activity

Look again at *Figure 7*, on p. 117. Add the concept 'values' to it, and draw arrows showing how they relate to the factors that are already there.

It is my view that sociology does not and cannot provide final answers and ultimate truths about the social world, for they do not exist. Sociology is a way of looking at the world which tries to develop new insights by approaching familiar questions from an unfamiliar angle. There is no single reality waiting to be discovered, no one right answer waiting to be found. The test of sociology is how far it helps us to understand the social world, for understanding and knowledge are the foundations of effective action. It will be more successful in doing this if research is done according to principles of integrity and rationality. Choice of topic to study will be value-laden, but methods must avoid all personal bias and in this sense should be value-free. The use to which any knowledge is put is a profoundly moral issue which sociologists, like other scientists, must not evade.

Appendix
Reading sociological research

A sociological research report should always include an account of how the research was done. If it does not, the reader cannot assess the merits of the research. Most books do contain such an account, and these should be read very carefully. They are usually in an early chapter, or in an Appendix. Virtually every study mentioned in this book includes one.

The account that the researcher gives will make many points explicitly, all of which should be carefully noted, but many will be only implicit, and it is important that these are identified and brought into the open. In addition, the reader must be on the alert for what has been left out in this official version of what happened (see p. 121).

The most important implicit assumptions are usually those that the researcher makes about the nature of what is being studied – social reality. Within this assumption is a model of man and of society, and of the relationship between them. The debate about positivist and interpretive research methods centres on these assumptions (see pp. 108–10).

So, when you are reading a research report, and especially the section about methods, you should ask yourself the following questions. Does the writer answer them, either explicitly or implicitly? If not, why do you think this is?

Remember that not every one of these questions applies to every research study.

Why did the researcher choose to study this topic?

Is there any indication of whether the results are likely to be 'useful' in some way? Perhaps in relation to some aspect of social policy? Or is it more a matter of description? Was the researcher trying to discover causes? Or just describe a social context? Or increase our understanding? Or a mixture of these?

Who was the research done for? Does the author suggest that the subjects of the research stand to gain from it in any way?

What were the circumstances in which the choice of topic was made, and the research done? Was it a lone researcher, perhaps working for a Ph.D.? Or a researcher with substantial backing from an institution? Was there a team of researchers? Was the research part of a wider programme? Was it a mixture of these?

How was the research paid for?

Do you think that this affected the choice of research topic, or the way the research was carried out? Or how it was reported?

What were the research methods used?

Why were these methods chosen? How far were they dictated by the topic of the research? Could any other methods have been used to study the same topic?

How was access gained to the subjects of the research?

Did anybody's permission have to be asked? Could the subjects of the research have refused to be studied? Did the researcher get to know the people being studied? If so, how?

Does the study use all primary data, or secondary data, or both?

If secondary data is involved, how is it used?

Is there any clear preference for survey methods, or for ethnographic methods, or for experiments?

If there is such a preference, is it explained or justified? How?

Does the researcher operationalize any concepts?

If so, which ones? And how?

Does the researcher discuss problems of objectivity, bias, and value-freedom?

What does the author seem to mean by these terms? How are the problems dealt with? Whose side does the researcher seem to be on? Anybody's? Or does it seem to be a neutral and objective account?

Is there a discussion of whether the research is scientific?

What does the researcher seem to mean by the term 'scientific'?

Is the question of representativeness raised?

If it is, is representativeness or typicality claimed? Is sampling discussed or described? If so, what kind of sampling is it?

Is the question of validity discussed?

How does the researcher claim validity, if at all?
   Does the researcher discuss the effect that the research may have had on the people being studied?

Is the question of reliability discussed?

Do you think that, if someone else had done the research, they would have come up with a similar account? If not, why not?

Does the researcher discuss any ethical problems raised by the research?

Are there problems of secrecy, or of anonymity? Is there any question of the subjects of the research suffering any hurt or disadvantage as a result of the research being published?

How is evidence presented?

Is it mainly in quantitative form, in tables and graphs? Or in qualitative form, with many quotations direct from those studied? Or is there a mixture of these, and are they used to complement each other?

If the research is mainly of the survey type, what does the researcher say about:

Sampling methods; questionnaire design; training interviewers and standardizing interviews; doing a pilot survey; data analysis?

Is the questionnaire reproduced in the book? What do you think of the questions? Are they clear? Unambiguous? Are they the right questions? What other questions would you have asked?

If the research is mainly of the ethnographic type, what does the researcher say about:

Joining the group being studied; adopting a role that is acceptable to the group; overt or covert research; leaving the group; 'going native'?

What has been left out of the account of how the research was done?

How frank and honest do you think the researcher has been in this account? Do you think the research really went as described? What other problems would you expect the researcher to have had?

How might a researcher with different theoretical assumptions have tackled this research?

What methods might have been used? How might the results have differed?

Above all, do you have a clear idea of why this research topic was chosen? Why these methods were adopted? How the research was carried out? And how the conclusions were reached? Do you have any view on whether the research report gives a true picture?

References

Argyle, M. (1959) *Religious Behaviour*. London: Routledge & Kegan Paul.

Atkinson, J.M. (1978) *Discovering Suicide: Studies in the Social Organization of Sudden Death*. London: Macmillan.

Becker, H.S. (1963) *Outsiders: Studies in the Sociology of Deviance*. New York: The Free Press.

—— (1967) Whose side are we on? *Social Problems*: 14.

Becker, H.S., Geer, B., Hughes, E.C., and Strauss, A.L. (1961) *Boys in White*. Chicago: University of Chicago Press.

Becker, H.S., Geer, B., and Hughes, E.C. (1968) *Making the Grade*. New York: Wiley.

Bell, C. and Newby, H. (1971) *Community Studies*. London: George Allen & Unwin.

Bell, C. and Newby, H. (1977) *Doing Sociological Research*. London: George Allen & Unwin.

Benson, S. (1981) *Ambiguous Ethnicity. Interracial Families in London*. Cambridge: Cambridge University Press.

Berger, P. and Luckmann, T. (1967) *The Social Construction of Reality*. Harmondsworth: Penguin.

Blauner, R. (1964) *Alienation and Freedom*. Chicago: University of Chicago Press.

Bott, E. (1971) *Family and Social Network*. London: Tavistock.

Burgess, R.G. (1982) *Field Research: A Sourcebook and Field Manual*. London: George Allen & Unwin.

Cohen, S. and Taylor, L. (1972) *Psychological Survival. The Experience of Long Term Imprisonment*. Harmondsworth: Penguin.

Corrigan, P. (1979) *Schooling the Smash Street Kids*. London: Macmillan.

Cuff, E.C. and Payne, G.C.F. (1984) *Perspectives in Sociology*. London: George Allen & Unwin.

Dalton, M. (1959) *Men Who Manage*. New York: Wiley.

Ditton, J. (1977) *Part-time Crime: An Ethnography of Fiddling and Pilferage*. London: Macmillan.

Douglas, J.W.B. (1964) *The Home and the School*. London: MacGibbon & Kee.

—— (1968) *All Our Future*. London: Peter Davies.

Durkheim, E. (1897) *Suicide: A Study in Sociology*. London: Routledge & Kegan Paul (1970).

Edgell, S. (1980) *Middle-class Couples*. London: George Allen & Unwin.

Eysenck, H.J. and Nias, D. (1978) *Sex, Violence and the Media*. London: Maurice Temple Smith.

Festinger, L., Rieken, N., and Schachter, P. (1956) *When Prophecy Fails*. New York: Harper & Row.

Flanders, N.A. (1970) *Analysing Teaching Behaviour*. New York: Addison Wesley.

Frankenberg, R. (1957) *Village on the Border*. London: Cohen & West.

—— (1966) *Communities in Britain*. Harmondsworth: Penguin.

Freeman, D. (1984) *Margaret Mead and Samoa. The making and unmaking of an anthropological myth*. Harmondsworth: Penguin.

Gans, H.J. (1962) *The Urban Villagers*. New York: The Free Press.

—— (1967) *The Levittowners*. London: Allen Lane.

Gavron, H. (1966) *The Captive Wife*. London: Routledge & Kegan Paul.

Glasgow University Media Group (1976) *Bad News*. London: Routledge & Kegan Paul.

Glueck, S. and Glueck, E. (1964) *Ventures in Criminology*. London: Tavistock.

Gold, R.L. (1958) Roles in Sociological Field Observation. *Social Forces* 6.

Goldthorpe, J.H., Lockwood, D., Bechhofer, F., and Platt, J. (1969) *The Affluent Worker in the Class Structure*. Cambridge: Cambridge University Press.

Goldthorpe, J.H. *et al.* (1980) *Social Mobility and Class Structure*. Oxford: The Clarendon Press.

Gomm, R. and McNeill, P. (1982) *Handbook for Sociology Teachers*. London: Heinemann.

Gouldner, A.W. (1973) *For Sociology: Renewal and Critique in Sociology Today*. Harmondsworth: Penguin.

Griffin, J.H. (1962) *Black Like Me*. London: Collins.

Halsey, A.H., Heath, A.F., and Ridge, J.M. (1980) *Origins and Destinations: Family, Class and Education in Modern Britain*. Oxford: The Clarendon Press.

Hammond, P. (1964) *Sociologists at Work*. New York: Basic Books.

Haney, C., Banks, C., and Zimbardo, P. (1973) *A Study of Prisoners and Guards in a Simulated Prison*. Reprinted in Potter *et al.* (1981).

Hargreaves, D. (1967) *Social Relations in a Secondary School*. London: Routledge & Kegan Paul.

Harris, M. (1984) The Strange Saga of the Video Bill. *New Society*, 26 April.

Humphreys, L. (1970) *Tea Room Trade*. London: Duckworth.

Keating, P. (1976) *Into Unknown England. Selections from the Social Explorers*. London: Fontana.

Kuhn, T.S. (1970) *The Structure of Scientific Revolutions*. Chicago: University of Chicago Press.

Lacey, C. (1970) *Hightown Grammar*. Manchester: Manchester University Press.

Lane, T. and Roberts, K. (1971) *Strike at Pilkingtons*. London: Collins.

Lewis, O. (1964) *The Children of Sanchez*. New York: Random House.

—— (1968) *La Vida*. London: Panther.

Liebow, E. (1967) *Tally's Corner*. London: Routledge & Kegan Paul.

Lipset, S.M. and Bendix, R. (1959) *Social Mobility in Industrial Society*. Berkeley: University of California Press.

Lynd, R.S. and Lynd, H.M. (1929) *Middletown: a Study in Contemporary American Culture*. New York: Harcourt Brace.

Lynd, R.S. and Lynd, H.M. (1937) *Middletown in Transition*. New York: Harcourt Brace.

131

McNeill, P. and Townley, C. (1981) *Fundamentals of Sociology*. London: Hutchinson.

Malinowski, B. (1967) *A Diary in the Strict Sense of the Term*. London: Routledge & Kegan Paul.

Mead, M. (1935) *Sex and Temperament in Three Primitve Societies*. New York: William Morrow.

Milgram, S. (1965) Some Conditions of Obedience and Disobedience to Authority. *Human Relations* 18: 57–74.

Newby, H. (1977) *The Deferential Worker*. London: Allen Lane.

Newson, J. and Newson, E. (1963) *Infant Care in an Urban Community*. London: George Allen & Unwin.

—— (1968) *Four Years Old in an Urban Community*. London: George Allen & Unwin.

Oakley, A. (1979) *From Here to Maternity*. Harmondsworth: Penguin.

Okely, J. (1983) *The Traveller-Gypsies*. Cambridge: Cambridge University Press.

Osborn, A.F., Butler, N.R., and Morris, A.C. (1984) *The Social Life of Britain's Five Year Olds*. London: Routledge & Kegan Paul.

Pahl, J.M. and Pahl, R.E. (1971) *Managers and Their Wives*. London: Allen Lane.

Parker, H.J. (1974) *View from the Boys*. Newton Abbot: David & Charles.

Patrick, J. (1973) *A Glasgow Gang Observed*. London: Eyre Methuen.

Pearson, D. (1981) *Race, Class and Political Activism. A Study of West Indians in Britain*. Farnborough: Gower.

Plant, M.A. (1975) *Drugtakers in an English Town*. London: Tavistock.

Polsky, N. (1967) *Hustlers, Beats and Others*. New York: Aldine.

Potter, D. and Sarre, P. (1974) *Dimensions of Society*. London: University of London Press/The Open University.

Potter, D., Anderson, J., Clarke, J., Coombes, P., Hall, S., Harris, L., Holloway, C., and Walton, T. (1981) *Society and the Social Sciences: An Introduction*. London: Routledge & Kegan Paul/The Open University.

Pryce, K. (1979) *Endless Pressure*. Harmondsworth: Penguin.

Rapoport, R. and Rapoport, R. (1971) *Dual Career Families*. Harmondsworth: Pelican.

Reid, I. (1981) *Social Class Differences in Britain*. London: Grant McIntyre.

132

Roberts, K., Cook, F.G., Clarke, S.C., and Semeonoff, E. (1977) *The Fragmentary Class Structure*. London: Heinemann.

Roberts, R. (1971) *The Classic Slum*. Manchester: University of Manchester Press.

Rosenhan, D.L. (1973) On Being Sane in Insane Places. *Science*.

Runciman, W.G. (1966) *Relative Deprivation and Social Justice*. London: Routledge & Kegan Paul.

Schofield, M. (1965) *The Sexual Behaviour of Young People*. Harlow: Longman.

Shaw, C. (1930) *The Jack-Roller: A Delinquent Boy's Own Story*. Chicago: University of Chicago Press.

Shipman, M. (1976) *The Organization and Impact of Social Research*. London: Routledge & Kegan Paul.

Sissons, M. (1970) *The Psychology of Social Class*. Bletchley: The Open University Press.

Stacey, M. (1960) *Tradition and Change: A Study of Banbury*. Oxford: Oxford University Press.

—— (1975) *Power, Persistence and Change: A Second Study of Banbury*. London: Routledge & Kegan Paul.

Thomas, W.I. and Znaniecki, F. (1919) *The Polish Peasant in Europe and America*. Chicago: University of Chicago Press.

Townsend, P. (1957, 1963) *The Family Life of Old People*. London: Routledge & Kegan Paul; Harmondsworth: Pelican.

—— (1979) *Poverty in the United Kingdom*. Harmondsworth: Penguin.

Townsend, P. and Davidson, N. (1982) *Inequalities in Health. The Black Report*. Harmondsworth: Penguin.

Whyte, W.F. (1955) *Street Corner Society*. Chicago: University of Chicago Press.

Willis, P. (1977) *Learning to Labour*. Farnborough: Saxon House.

Willmott, P. (1966) *Adolescent Boys of East London*. London: Routledge & Kegan Paul.

Willmott, P. and Young, M. (1960) *Family and Class in a London Suburb*. London: Routledge & Kegan Paul.

Worsley, P. (1977) *Introducing Sociology*. Harmondsworth: Penguin.

Young, M. and Willmott, P. (1957) *Family and Kinship in East London*. London: Routledge & Kegan Paul.

—— (1973) *The Symmetrical Family*. London: Routledge & Kegan Paul.

Index

135